The Secrets of Discipline

Reset Your Mind and Achieve the Unimaginable

Paola Knecht

Knecht Publishing

Contents

Disclaimer vii
Introduction xi

Part One | Know Your Enemy

Chapter 1 | Instant Gratification 5
Chapter 2 | Procrastination 7
Chapter 3 | Mediocrity 10
Chapter 4 | Social Media 13
Chapter 5 | Toxic Foods 18
Chapter 6 | The Traditional Educational System 24
Chapter 7 | Interpersonal Relationships 32
Chapter 8 | Fear 42

Part Two | Reprogram your mind

Chapter 9 | The Power of Self-Awareness 49
Chapter 10 | Determination 53
Chapter 11 | A Resilient Mind 57
Chapter 12 | Staying Alert 60
Chapter 13 | Motivation 63
Chapter 14 | Vision 66
Chapter 15 | Focus 69
Chapter 16 | Silence 72
Chapter 17 | Stabilize Your Emotions 76
Chapter 18 | Powerful Reprogramming Methods 80

Part Three | Establish Systems

Chapter 19 | Powerful Routines 89
Chapter 20 | The Power of Microtasks 93
Chapter 21 | Create a Winning System 96
Chapter 22 | Throw Away the Concept of "Multitasking" 104

Chapter 23 | Visualize the Practice Before Executing 108
Chapter 24 | Fall in Love with the Process 111
Chapter 25 | The Magic of the Subconscious 115
I'd Love Your Feedback 119
About the Author 121

Bibliography 123

Knecht Publishing

Cover illustration and design: David Colón

Proofreading and comprehensive editing: Julián Chappa

Disclaimer

This book details the personal experiences and opinions of the author regarding mental and physical health. However, neither the author nor this book is a substitute for your trusted healthcare provider.

We emphasize that this book is not a replacement for consultations with a licensed healthcare professional, such as your physician. Before starting any health program or making lifestyle changes, you should consult your doctor or another qualified healthcare professional to ensure that you are in good health and that the examples provided in this book will be beneficial to you.

This volume contains content related to physical and/or mental health issues. By using this book, you accept this disclaimer as a reader.

For those striving to create a better world.

Introduction

Do you feel like time is passing faster than usual? You're not alone. Our modern society moves at a dizzying pace, to the point where it feels like time is running at "2x" speed.

Suddenly, your hours slip away, and each evening you find yourself wondering, "Where did the whole day go?" And another day passes, another week, another month, another year... leaving us with a long list of things to do and dreams to fulfill. Time simply isn't enough.

This fast-paced lifestyle is pushing us to take on a load of activities and social expectations that are incompatible with our *natural* life rhythm.

Just a few decades ago, our way of life was much slower. We took the time to communicate with others in a proper and cordial way, for example, through handwritten letters.

Receiving a letter written by hand excited us. We took time to read it, and then sat down in silence to write a thoughtful response, which we would leave at the post office and wait weeks, sometimes months, to receive another letter in reply.

The wait was as sweet as it was thrilling. Sometimes intriguing. We delighted in waiting for news from our loved ones. How many artists—composers, writers, or painters—were inspired to create their art in that empty space, in the anticipation of the sweet wait?

Now, that no longer exists. The culture of immediacy, gradually taking hold since the year 2000, has completely changed our social and cultural dynamics. We all have to be available 24/7 on WhatsApp.

We don't even have to write anymore; now, emojis solve part of the communication. We receive news from multiple sources, instantly, all the time. We live in the age of hyperstimulation and hyperconnectivity.

Now, you may wonder: what does this have to do with discipline? More than you think! As good strategists, we must carefully study the battlefield and understand what we're up against.

We all have dreams. We all want to achieve our goals, big or small. Some dream of financial freedom to travel and enjoy life, others of getting married and starting a family, others perhaps dream of becoming millionaires or landing their dream job at a big company.

No matter what your goal or dream is, to achieve it you need to operate—at least in this reality—in the dimension of space-time.

You need energy.

You need to give yourself the space and time to execute.

You need to stop and think clearly, map out a route, and follow it.

And in this reality we live in, amid the frenzy of immediacy, things become quite complicated. So no, dear reader... I won't blame you for your lack of discipline. If you've picked up this book, it's because you're seeking ways to become more disciplined to improve your life.

By now, we have countless sources of information—books, podcasts, videos, courses, and endless products—that promise to help us develop steel discipline and become the next David Goggins* or Serena Williams.

The intentions are good, but we can't ignore what we're up against, which is a social construct designed precisely to prevent us from achieving true discipline.

Modern society and the way we live day-to-day today definitely don't help us have discipline. On social media, we're bombarded by *influencers* and all kinds of individuals boasting about an idyllic life full of travel, luxury, and fun, claiming that "It's not necessary to work hard to achieve abundance and a dream life." You only need to consume their content and buy their 21-day abundance method "with just one click," and *voilà!*

However, reality looks very different in the light of day. You sign up for abundance podcasts, consume trendy influencer content, but in the end, most people end up the same: they get motivated for the first days or weeks... and then quit. Why is it so difficult to master this simple and mysterious art of developing consistent, lasting discipline?

My proposal with this book is to show you three things in brief yet relevant chapters:

1. The lack of discipline is not entirely your fault.
2. We live in a mental prison imposed by multiple fronts (including our society and culture), which prevent us from exploring our full potential.
3. Good news! You can change your reality and train your mind to achieve everything you dream of, even if it means going against the current.

I have often asked myself:

Why is it that the majority of people live frustrated, unhappy,

* Ultramarathon runner, cyclist, triathlete, public speaker, and author.

seemingly incapable of achieving their dreams and personal fulfillment?

Why is it that only a very small percentage of humanity is able to "push their limits" and achieve true fulfillment in their lives?

What is the superpower these people have to achieve their dreams, and how can we make it accessible to everyone?

No, I don't believe it's just discipline. At least, it's not the only superpower.

It's also not about blindly following what trendy influencers say. The real power lies in the fact that people who succeed in their personal fulfillment operate in a reality-consciousness that they create for themselves. They free themselves from the mental prison.

Freeing yourself from the prison is the goal and the key. And one of the keys to opening the prison is habit and mental discipline.

I count myself among those people who desperately sought a method, a formula, to succeed in everything I dreamed of: in my profession as an engineer, mentor, author, being an excellent mother, a good wife, a friend, exercising, and having quality time to enjoy the beautiful things life has to offer.

And no matter how much I meticulously planned and filled agendas, and no matter how many books I read, listened to experts, or recited my daily affirmations... I failed! Structuring my day like a military schedule wasn't enough. Being part of the 5 a.m. club, listening to podcasts, and reading non-stop didn't work for me.

Something I personally felt was missing was seeing more female authors publishing their effective methods for developing good discipline. Somehow, there's a lot of material written by men, especially in this area, and I found many authors who were part of Special Forces, athletes, or men who went from being unemployed to building their own businesses, etc.

I've learned very valuable things from them, but I won't deny that constantly—while reading their advice—I found myself asking: How do you follow these tips when you're a woman juggling small children, a husband, a household, a corporate job, and the dreams of becoming a writer, painter, or entrepreneur — all while trying to make time for exercise, self-care, and healthy eating?

How do you develop good discipline without having to wake up at 4 a.m., run 10 kilometers first thing in the morning, or spend six hours at the gym training, only to work until 2 a.m. so you can write or build your own business?

That's when I realized that we need more women to share their secrets on how they solve this mysterious puzzle of wanting to do everything at once. I felt I had to contribute my small piece to this subject and started testing every possible method. Exhausted by not getting results, I decided to give up for the moment, and that's when I realized my true challenge. I had to escape from my own prison and stop being the agent of my own destruction.

In this book, I share everything I learned on my journey to break free and find the balance I had been desperately seeking — a balance that has worked wonders for me. My hope is that it will help you escape your own prison, or at the very least, allow you to glimpse the beautiful light filtering through the bars... the promise of true freedom, the kind you've been dreaming of.

I hope I've convinced you to at least give it a try. If so... let's get to work!

Part One | Know Your Enemy

"Though we like to believe we are free, many of us are trapped in a mental prison of our own making. Our most ruthless jailer is our unhealthy inner dialogue, that relentless inner critic which brutally sabotages us with nagging doubts and harsh judgments."

—MARCUS AURELIUS, *Meditations*

To master any skill, it's essential to recognize your limitations. A lack of awareness about our boundaries is our true adversary. To me, this is a crucial point because it compels us to face the enemy directly.

When I trained in coaching techniques, facilitators loved using the concept of "limiting beliefs." One of the first things a *coach* asks a client when they describe their situation is, "What do you think is holding you back from achieving this or that?" Clients often respond, "Fear, shame, or the belief that I can't do it."

In my view, these conversations remain on the surface because most coaches hesitate to go beyond the supposed "limiting beliefs" their clients think they have.

Few coaches, mentors, influencers, or similar professionals truly grasp the underlying reasons why people—especially in today's world—remain confined within their own realities, perceiving them as limited, challenging, and beyond their control.

In truth, problems don't exist as such. Everything we perceive externally results from an interaction of information and energy vibrating at specific frequencies that our brains interpret and project as a holographic image.

It might sound like science fiction, but an increasing number of scientists support this view of reality. Mexican scientist Carlos Grinberg-Zylberbaum, in his syntergic theory, argues that the space we perceive as empty and lacking fundamental structure is, in fact, rich with information. According to his theory, every point in space contains the total information of all other points, structured in perfect geometric harmony. He calls this spatial structure the "*Lattice*," which is also referred to as the "Matrix."

This Lattice or Matrix has an extraordinary capacity to store all the information of the universe within each of its points. In simpler terms, our retina, though millimeters in size, can decode the neuro-algorithms of the Lattice. What we perceive is the result of our brain's capacity to decode and interpret reality.

In essence, everything you see contains the entirety of the universe's information. However, your level of consciousness acts as a filter, allowing you to perceive only what the filter permits.

Understanding this is crucial because it reveals that our "reality" is simply an interpretation of energy and information within the neural field that our brains decode. Practically speaking: "What you believe is what you see."

With this perspective, let me introduce you to the primary

enemies we face. Some are mental by nature, while others manifest as "external influences" or interferences.

Chapter 1 | Instant Gratification

Our craving for constant pleasure isn't a product of social media or the internet, though these tools have undoubtedly amplified the problem. Today, entire industries exploit this aspect of human psychology to keep us hooked and sell us endless products and services.

Advertising campaigns bombard us with promises of quick fixes: the shampoo that will give you flawless hair, the medicine that instantly cures your fatigue, the detergent that erases the toughest stains, or the perfume that magically enhances your allure. These "miracle products" lure us in, only for us to realize later that the solution often creates new problems—and the cycle repeats.

The real issue isn't the products themselves; some are genuinely helpful. The problem lies in how this constant bombardment erodes our ability to trust our intuition and think critically about what we consume. We've been conditioned to seek instant solutions rather than invest the time and effort required to truly understand and address our needs.

Take hair care as an example. Rather than putting in the effort to understand what our hair needs, we fall for flashy ads and buy products claiming "natural extracts" but filled with chemicals. True hair care, like any meaningful goal—be it weight loss, fitness, or professional success—requires structure, discipline, and consistent effort. Yet, in our fast-paced lives, few are willing to commit to such a process.

The same principle applies to careers. Many people seek quick recognition through empty posturing—attending meetings to seem important, voicing opinions without offering solutions—rather than producing tangible results. This superficial approach may garner temporary attention but rarely contributes lasting value.

Instant gratification is a societal cancer that undermines the building of anything worthwhile. Great civilizations and meaningful achievements are not created overnight. They require patience, dedication, and an alignment of thought and action over time.

Moreover, our environments increasingly reflect this obsession with immediacy. Cities are designed less for reflection or quiet contemplation and more for entertainment and consumption. This lack of space for deep thought leaves little room for genuine personal growth or long-term planning.

In essence, our addiction to quick fixes hinders us from constructing lives of lasting value and quality. Whether it's choosing to splurge on a trendy vacation for Instagram likes or investing in a business or property, our decisions ultimately reveal the level of consciousness we bring to our lives.

Chapter 2 | Procrastination

In our daily lives, we often focus on what feels urgent or even waste time on things that are neither important nor urgent (like checking social media every two minutes). Yet, we fail to invest in what *truly matters*.

Procrastination is a complex behavior influenced by many factors—an intrinsic fear of failure, lack of motivation, poor time management, feeling overwhelmed, mood swings, and more.

When you give your mind meaningful tasks during your waking hours, you'll feel more satisfied and at ease throughout the day, setting yourself up to start the next day on a relaxed note. This is far better than letting your mind aimlessly wander through the endless sea of information offered by the internet and social media.

I could fill an entire book with stories of people whose dreams crumbled because procrastination was their greatest enemy. This habit of postponing action—whether out of fear, laziness, or lack of motivation—is one of the most dangerous weapons we wield against ourselves. It's the classic "I'll start tomorrow," or worse,

"Now's not the right time." As if some perfect moment in the distant future actually exists.

When someone asks me, "Paola, when is the best time to take action (change jobs, start eating healthier, etc.)?"—regardless of the goal—my answer is always the same: ***Today!*** There is no better moment than now.

If you have a dream or a goal, the only time to work toward it is today. Tomorrow doesn't exist—it's a perpetual illusion. We live in an eternal present. Start today, or risk *never* starting at all.

"But how do I start today?" some clients ask me, skeptical that it's even possible. It's not just possible—it's the most powerful thing you can do for yourself if you truly want to change.

Starting doesn't mean taking a giant leap into the unknown. You can start small. We'll talk more about this method in later chapters. The worst thing you can do is not begin at all.

It's easier said than done, I know. Invisible forces often work against us. Some days, you'll feel unmotivated, tired, or unwell. Maybe you're going through a tough time in life and tell yourself, *"I don't have the energy for this today; I'll feel better tomorrow."* But when tomorrow arrives, you'll likely find another excuse—sound familiar?

As David Goggins—ultramarathon runner, cyclist, triathlete, public speaker, and author—says: *"The most important thing is to push yourself to the max when you most feel like giving up because that's what strengthens your mind to its fullest. That's why you must do your best work when you feel the least motivated."*

Procrastinating is tempting and easy when you lack passion—a fire inside you that refuses to give up. It's far easier to come up with excuses and stay in the comfort of your warm, cozy zone. But the problem is that this habit will keep you stuck in a victim mindset and mediocrity, preventing you from moving forward.

Do you really want to discover who you are and what you're

capable of? Then you need to break free from the *"I'll start tomorrow"* mentality as quickly as possible.

How do you deal with fear? You obliterate it. Later on, we'll discuss how to train your mind to destroy any attempts by your lower self—your protective ego—that wants to keep you as a tiny bonsai tree that never grows. Strengthen your roots, and grow toward the sky!

Chapter 3 | Mediocrity

"In a society where mediocrity is too often the standard and too frequently rewarded, there is an intense fascination with men who despise mediocrity, who refuse to define themselves in conventional terms, and who seek to transcend traditionally recognized human abilities."

—DAVID GOGGINS

Our modern society celebrates mediocrity. Just look around, and you'll see that the law of least effort dominates our lives. Combined with instant gratification, this creates a dangerous cocktail, a seemingly benign environment that turns into one of the biggest enemies of discipline.

Discipline requires constant commitment, sustained effort over long periods of time. It demands focus, questioning limits, and being unshakable in our determination despite the apparent setbacks and rejections we may encounter along the way.

Mediocrity is celebrated by governments and big industries

(yes, even by them) and is even supported by the current education system. Why? Simple: because a person who is content with small things poses no threat to those in power.

Being mediocre means staying in your little cage, settling for what you have, and not aspiring for more. I know these words hurt because it's not easy to accept that the majority of people live in small cages, designed so comfortably that we hardly realize we're inside invisible bars.

Why is this bad for developing good **self-discipline**? Simply put, staying comfortable in a "safe" place will get you nowhere. Developing good self-discipline requires feeling an internal fire strong enough to want to move from where you are. If you don't have that inner fire and feel comfortable where you are, how do you expect your situation to change?

Now, I don't criticize people who choose not to move from where they are. That's perfectly acceptable for some. This book is for those who do want to do more with their lives, for those who want to explore how far they can truly go.

The human spirit, if not manipulated, has no limits. Not even physical barriers can stop a person who is willing to change their reality. I touched on this point when we mentioned Jacobo Grinberg-Zylberbaum's syntergic theory. He claims that we cannot discover how consciousness arises from matter simply because matter does not exist. Only different degrees of consciousness exist.

A human being who has been raised in a punitive environment where feelings of guilt are constantly manipulated conceives themselves as bad or "undeserving," incapable of achieving something extraordinary like complete happiness.

Once you surpass that primitive level of consciousness where fear dominates, you can truly create your own reality. The invisible barriers fade away because, in reality, they never existed.

The decision is yours. What do you want to do with your life?

Are you willing to break through those invisible cages and liberate yourself into a reality where all your dreams are possible?

Chapter 4 | Social Media

Social media can be fabulous when we use it to our advantage, as we are literally "one click" away from interacting with a vast number of people. Having a Facebook, Instagram, or X (formerly Twitter) account instantly democratizes access to all kinds of information. You can find out about the latest news from all over the world in seconds from multiple sources. Traditional channels like newspapers, TV stations, and other mass media have lost their power and prestige as the sole sources of information. Now, anyone can access all kinds of news, without waiting for traditional media to publish something.

Despite the clear benefits of having information at our fingertips, there are consequences, and the price is not cheap. When we talk about **discipline,** we refer to the ability to focus on a task for a long enough time to achieve the desired result. In today's society, this ability seems to be in danger of extinction.

Everyone wants everything instantly, with the least effort possible. Accessing platforms like TikTok, where the most viral videos last only a few seconds and you can literally spend hours watching hundreds of entertaining clips, sounds amazing to many.

But over time, it destroys our ability to concentrate or reduces our tolerance for boredom, leading many teens today to aspire only to easy, temporary jobs—preferably working from home or as influencers.

Social media platforms are designed to be highly addictive, generating high levels of dopamine each time we interact with them and receive instant gratifications like likes, comments, and followers. It's a little narcissistic empire where the only purpose of using social media is to attract attention, sharing photos of what you eat, your travels, meetings with friends and family, the cool concert you went to over the weekend, and other such things.

But what is the real benefit of sharing so much private information on social media? Attention? Fame? Social acceptance? The consequence is that, at the end of the day, it creates an addiction to sharing and consuming content to the point where valuable hours of your time are lost while you're trapped in social media, without having actually created anything valuable for your life.

Cal Newport, author and professor of Computer Science, warns in his book *Deep Work* that using social media and the internet for entertainment can have negative consequences on our mental health and overall well-being. Newport argues that when we don't give our minds high-value, quality work to focus on, they start absorbing all kinds of information, even junk information we don't need.

This results in feeling exhausted and empty after a social media marathon, a sense that only disappears when we go back to scrolling on our screens for more of the same.

Twenge & Campbell (2018) found a significant association between increased time spent on social media screens and profound states of depression in teens. Another study by Fardouly, Diedrichs, et al. (2015) explored the relationship between Instagram use and negative body image, revealing that people who spent more time on this platform were more likely to make social comparisons between their own lives and what they saw on Instagram, which led to a negative perception of their own bodies and low self-esteem.

Now, think about how you're using this precious gift from God: the ability to shape your life at any given moment. Is it really worth spending hours watching fun videos on TikTok and Facebook? Is it really worth spending hours and hours in front of Netflix watching your favorite series?

A recent study by Al Jazeera* (2023) revealed that in 2023, around 4.8 billion users used social media daily. That's 60% of the world's population! An interesting aspect of the study is that it analyzed the platforms where people spend the most time. Not surprisingly, Facebook took the top spot with 2.9 billion users, followed by YouTube with 2.5 billion; WhatsApp and Instagram were tied for third place with 2 billion users each; TikTok had 1.05 billion; and WeChat (China's version of WhatsApp) had 1.4 billion users.

Another interesting fact is how much time active users spend on these platforms daily. The report revealed that the typical user spends an average of 2.5 hours a day on social media—equivalent to 864 hours a year, simply scrolling through apps. That's basically over a month a year just consuming information on social media!

Being constantly connected to social media produces a relatively new effect in this era of hyper-digital connectivity: *FOMO* (Fear of Missing Out). This effect on the human psyche is associated with numerous cases of anxiety and depression. This false sense that real life happens on social media makes people feel that if they're not connected all the time, they're "missing out" on something—whether it's the news of the moment, a friend's vaca-

* ALI, Marium (2023): «How many years does a typical user spend on social media?».Available on: www.aljazeera.com/news/2023/6/30/how-many-years-does-a-typical-user-spend-on-social-media#.

tion photos, a colleague's latest gym visit, or the latest drama about a celebrity.

It's truly sad to see how we waste this precious gift—time—on things that have negative repercussions for our physical and mental health. However, we know that the world is increasingly focused on creating a virtual life on social media. Do we have any alternatives?

While it's true that everything today moves through the internet and social media, and that if you want to prosper in your business or career you need some exposure to the digital world, it's also true that we can do this more consciously and in a more structured way.

For example, one method that has worked well for me is to reserve one hour a day exclusively for checking emails, browsing the internet, and using social media. When I plan my day, I make a list of things I need to do on the internet: write emails, do some shopping, research a topic, or check my social networks.

During that hour, I do everything I need to do, and once the time is up, I turn off my computer or set my phone aside. I feel better following this method because my mind "feels at peace" knowing I've done everything I needed to do, and I don't have to worry about it for the rest of the day.

Another important point: when you're doing something that requires a lot of concentration, turn off your phone. Receiving notifications all the time—whether by sound or vibration—immediately disrupts your ability to focus, and the risk of interrupting what you're doing to check notifications is high. It's better to eliminate that risk completely by turning off your phone and stopping the constant bombardment.

If you want to cure yourself of the "addiction" caused by social media use and give your life more quality time and attention, offer your mind higher-quality alternatives: replace or limit social media use with a good book, go for a walk and listen to a motivational or enriching podcast, start a project where you use your hands more —like painting, knitting, decorating a space, mountain biking, etc. The possibilities are rich and varied. Your mind and your health will thank you for it.

Chapter 5 | Toxic Foods

"Food and drinks change your emotions, thoughts, and the way you perceive the world."
—DAVID PERLMUTTER, *Brain Wash*

You've probably heard the well-meaning saying, "You are what you eat," and it's absolutely true. Just like everything in the universe, food is also energy. Every meal we consume has a direct impact on both our physical and mental health.

If we want to be disciplined individuals, we need optimal energy. Without energy, it's impossible to carry out our daily tasks efficiently.

Ultraprocessed foods, fluoride-laced water, the soil where our food grows, polluted with fertilizers, meats laden with antibiotics and chemicals, the synthetic materials of the clothes that touch your skin—everything has a negative impact when absorbed into our bodies.

Toxic food is a silent enemy. It may seem harmless, but it's quite treacherous. What's wrong with having a donut every now and then? If I come home from work and feel tired, why not just order a burger from McDonald's or a pizza, avoiding the hassle of cooking?

It's a reasonable excuse, but I doubt you'll feel like going for a run in the park or working on your projects after eating a burger or pizza. Chances are, the next thing you'll do is turn on the TV and binge-watch a series. Or perhaps start scrolling through social media, checking what you missed in the last 30 seconds that you didn't check your phone.

It's important to be aware of the negative effects of consuming **ultraprocessed food**. While we might not see the immediate consequences of eating pizza or a donut every night, the medium- and long-term effects are undeniable.

I understand that breaking the addiction to "junk food" is hard, and I don't blame you—it's designed to be addictive. Its trap lies in the instant gratification syndrome. When you're feeling down or "low on energy," eating a piece of cake might not seem like a bad idea. The sugar rush (dopamine) feels good—it calms you and makes you feel better, even if it's only for a short while.

The trap is that sugar is highly addictive, and your initial plan to eat just one piece of cake may turn into two or three more. Of course, while savoring the cake, you're not thinking about how sugar causes chronic inflammation, which negatively affects the brain, leading to more poor decisions and compulsive behavior.

Pay close attention to how this enemy operates, because food is one of the most powerful tools used by corporations and other power groups to keep humanity sick and drained of energy.

A healthy, dynamic, and vibrant person is not a good customer for McDonald's, Burger King, Pizza Hut, Starbucks, or Dunkin' Donuts. A person who feels good about themselves, who is happy and fulfilled, is not a good customer for malls or entertainment centers.

Someone at peace and in complete harmony with themselves doesn't need sleeping pills, nutritionists, the latest trendy diet, facial yoga, shopping sprees, cosmetic surgeries, or altering their body in any way.

Look closely, and you'll see that most commercial or "capitalist" activities thrive on human suffering and unhappiness in order to be profitable. The food sector is no exception. Yes, there's a market for healthy food, and many healthy alternatives exist.

The point here is that we must be aware of the central role food plays in our well-being. If we want to succeed in life and develop outstanding discipline to achieve the life we dream of, we must be fully conscious of the type of energy we're consuming through our food.

All the chemicals and processed substances we ingest cause inflammation. Inflammation leads to anxiety, and it's directly related to sleep deprivation in adults. An adult who doesn't sleep well produces large amounts of cortisol, the stress hormone.

If you wake up feeling tired, it's likely because you have high levels of cortisol in your body. It's proven that cortisol has depressive effects because it disrupts how our body produces and processes glucose, slowing down our metabolism. This results in a weakened immune system.

A decision that may seem insignificant, like eating a small donut, triggers a series of almost imperceptible events in both our body and mind—that's where its true danger lies. We can't take our nutrition lightly if we want to live a life that makes us feel happy and at peace.

Obviously, this applies equally to other addictions, like alcohol, tobacco, and other drugs. One "cigarette" a day may seem harmless, but if you smoke one cigarette every day for twenty years, we're talking about quantities the body simply can't tolerate.

Obesity doesn't develop "overnight."It's the result of a long process of poor decisions and eating habits that have built up over time. Awakening to the reality of our own consciousness can help us make better decisions about the food we offer our bodies and the decisions we make.

Everything is connected. In this reality, no link is alone. Your mind dictates what you eat, and what you eat dictates your physical health

We live in a holistic reality, where everything—even the smallest particle of air you breathe—is part of you. So, ultimately, the decision is yours. Will you continue letting others manipulate you through "junk food"? Are you ready to take control of your own choices and select your food wisely?

Perhaps your next reaction will be, "Okay, I get it, but if everything around us is contaminated with chemicals in the water, air, and soil, what's safe to eat?" That's a very good question, but unfortunately, there's no easy answer. We're all still searching for better food alternatives.

My recommendation is to always opt for the natural and organic, starting by frequenting stores that offer fresh, local products that aren't canned or have long expiration dates. Pay attention to what's available locally and look for organic alternatives. As much as possible, avoid large supermarkets and support local farmers. Your health, the environment, and your community will thank you.

It's not just about food...

There's growing concern in the manufacturing industry regarding products containing PFAS*. PFAS are a group of chemical substances that accumulate in both the human body and the envi-

---

* PFAS is the acronym for perfluoroalkyl and polyfluoroalkyl substances, a group

ronment and don't break down easily, making them permanent. They're often referred to as "forever chemicals."

There are an estimated 5,000 to 14,000 PFAS-related chemicals used for more than 50 years due to their high resistance to grease, water, fire, heat, and oil. They're used in food packaging, non-stick cookware, waterproof clothing, carpets, and even furniture.

The European Environment Agency (EEA) has shown through various studies that exposure to PFAS is linked to health problems such as liver damage, thyroid diseases, fertility issues, obesity, and even cancer.

I'm not mentioning this to cause panic or suggest that you leave the toxic social construct and move to a remote place without human presence to start your own self-sustaining system (although, on second thought, that's not a bad idea...).

My goal is simply to share with you what I know, and what I've seen over many years in industries where the focus has always been more on profit than on prioritizing human health.

As I mentioned earlier, disease brings enormous profits to countless industries. Wait... don't throw out all your pans or waterproof clothing yet! As we awaken, we'll encounter many unpleasant realities. No one likes the idea of knowing that much of what's sold in supermarkets is contaminated with harmful substances.

Our task is to be aware of this reality and at least do what we can to maintain our health in the best possible way, because knowledge is power.

It's worth being conscious of your purchases and trying to select products that are "PFAS-free" whenever possible. In the bibliography, you'll find a website where you can find PFAS-free

---

of chemical agents that includes PFOA, PFOS, GenX, and many other chemicals. For more information, visit EPA's PFAS page and PFAS Central.

products (it contains a list of brands for clothing, cosmetics, kitchenware, and more). As always, the decision is yours.

Chapter 6 | The Traditional Educational System

" Little boxes on the hillside
Little boxes made of ticky-tacky.
And the people in the houses
All went to the university
Where they were put in boxes
And they came out all the same.
And there's doctors and lawyers
And business executives
And they're all made of ticky-tacky
And they all look the same.
And the kids go to school, to the summer camp, and then to the university where they are put in boxes
And they come out all the same."

- MALVINA REYNOLDS, Little Boxes

This may seem controversial. How is it possible that the educational system, with its structure and rigidity, does not turn students into disciplined and empowered individuals? Isn't that one of the main benefits of the educational system?

I'm afraid, dear reader, that's not the case. One thing is to create standardized cardboard soldiers trained to follow orders and fear authority, and another very different thing is to train the mind to seek ways to expand, working hard and with steel resilience to achieve your goals, your dreams, even if to do so you must go against the society in which you live.

Traditional education defends the structure of society, governmental structures, and the status quo. It produces "civilized" people, capable of behaving in society, working as employees, and able to submit to all kinds of rules and policies to stay on the sidelines, receiving a mediocre salary but enough to provide, at best, a roof with a bed and hot food (at worst, continuing to keep the poorest on the margins, with miserable aid, and encouraging mediocrity with schools that lack even the most basic resources, but that's another topic).

I myself have been a victim of this system. Since I was a child, I was always very good at following rules, although I had my rebellious phase at the age of 8, when I couldn't find the point of following my teacher's orders regarding school tasks and activities. At that time, I preferred to go out in the afternoons to play and explore parks with my neighbors.

Multiplication tables and dividing numbers with three or more digits seemed quite trivial to me compared to my ghost-hunting games and the building of our "clubhouses" (huts) in the abandoned woods.

Until one day, my fourth-grade teacher almost failed me in Mathematics and very clearly told me, "You're bad at Math, if you keep this up, I don't see any good professional future for you." That message must have been deeply engraved in my soul, and I believe that to this day I am still trying to prove to that teacher that she was wrong. Perhaps unconsciously, that life sentence given by my teacher, "without meaning to," propelled me toward my decision to study Engineering.

Not only did I graduate as an Engineer, but I did so with honors. Although at the time I don't think I remembered my elementary school teacher, surely in my subconscious I wished to run into her and rub my degree in her face.

Finally, and here's the point I want to express with this particular story: I followed the rules of the game as best I could. I graduated as an Engineer, studied a Master's in International Business in Switzerland, and upon graduating and entering the "world of work," I realized I knew very well how to apply to companies and create an attractive résumé, but I had no idea how to start a business or how to make an effective sale.

I spent more than twenty years of my life "preparing for life," but in the end, with all that and my Master's in International Business, I didn't even know how to sell a sandwich to a stranger. So I asked myself:

How to survive in this world, living off my dreams?

I was taught that my dreams could only be hobbies, but if I wanted to "make a living," I had to pursue a career, work for companies, and earn a good salary.

When I wrote my first book, *The Success Mindset*, I researched a characteristic that was repeated, the common denominator of people who achieved success in their professions, as well as great satisfaction and fulfillment in their lives.

One of my discoveries, and something that caught my attention, is that the vast majority of those who were entrepreneurs — and became very successful with their businesses and professions — at some point left the educational system.

Some examples I researched were the case of Amancio Ortega, founder of the Inditex giant (a conglomerate that includes stores like Zara, Bershka, Pull & Bear, Massimo Dutti, etc.), who left school at 14 to work as a blouse maker in a small tailoring shop in his hometown of La Coruña (Spain). Ortega is now one of the richest men in the world.

In another field is the case of Alejandro Jodorowsky, a Chilean filmmaker, artist, writer, and tarot reader. He attended two years of university at the Pedagogical Institute in Santiago, Chile, but decided to drop out after hearing a professor say that human beings should adapt to the behavior of machines. He then decided to dedicate himself to theater. Today, at 95 years old, he is one of the most beloved, acclaimed, and versatile Spanish-speaking artists.

Swiss tennis legend Roger Federer, often considered the best tennis player of all time, also left school at 16 to fully pursue his true passion. I could continue listing hundreds of examples from various professions, such as author J. K. Rowling, acclaimed chef Anthony Bourdain, among others, but the point is clear: the educational system does not produce entrepreneurs; it mainly produces followers and employees. Following orders and being obedient to authority has nothing to do with discipline.

In his brilliant book *Dumbing Us Down*, John Taylor Gatto explains that he was a teacher in the United States education system for over 30 years, and during that time, he realized that today's education system doesn't educate you; it indoctrinates you. From his perspective, children shouldn't spend twelve years of their most valuable time locked up five days a week, nine months a year. Instead, we should instill in them the qualities of curiosity, adventure, resilience, the ability to research on their own, and reach their own conclusions; we should give them more autonomy in exploring how the world works.

But who came up with the idea of constructing this type of

system, which we now blindly entrust to our children and youth? None other than James Bryant Conant, who was president of Harvard University for twenty years, as well as holding other interesting positions, including being a poisonous gas specialist during World War I and a general executive for the atomic bomb project during World War II.

This figure was one of the most influential in the United States during the 20th century and a great promoter of implementing this system. The details can be found in his essay *The Child, The Parent and the State*, published in 1959, and its main message states that the modern school is the result of a "revolution"... A revolution of what exactly?

Bryant's intention, as explained by Alexander Inglis in his book *Principles of Secondary Education*, published in 1918, is to keep the masses controlled; by dividing children by subject, age, test results, and many other seemingly harmless means throughout their childhood and adolescence, the probability of humanity uniting into a "dangerous" mass is reduced. Remember the phrase *Divide et Impera*?

The more fragmented reality is perceived, the less likely humanity will realize the true nature of that reality. According to Bryant and Inglis, the true motives of modern compulsory education are as follows:

1. **Adaptive function**: Schools must establish fixed, repetitive habits of responding to authority. Children should not develop critical judgment. Obedience should be evaluated to see how much children can do silly and boring things without complaining.
2. **Integrative function**: This can also be called the "conformist" function because the aim is to make children as similar as possible. People who comply with everything are predictable and much easier to

manipulate. Perfect for forming an obedient workforce.

3. **Diagnostic and direction function**: The school must determine the appropriate role each student must play in society, keeping a "permanent record" of their abilities...
4. **Differentiating function**: Once the social role has been "diagnosed," children are separated by roles and categories according to the destiny they are expected to fulfill in the social "machine." Nothing more and nothing less.
5. **Selective function**: This has nothing to do with freedom of choice but with Darwin's theory of "natural selection" applied to favored races. Schools aim to categorize children who "don't measure up" and punish them with low grades, remedial classes, and other humiliating measures. This ensures that the "disobedient" experience, at an early age, the consequences of not obeying authority.
6. **Propedeutic function**: This is based on the fundamental idea of dividing education into several levels, starting with a generalized introductory level, followed by more specialized education. The social system that follows this type of structure requires an elite group to act as caretakers. To maintain this structure, only a small fraction of children are trained to manage this ongoing project in which the population remains deliberately and systematically dumbed down, continuing to generate obedient masses, fanatics, and a submissive workforce for large corporations.

Now, you may be wondering... well, what does it have to do

with the current education system being designed this way and the development of discipline?

More than you can imagine.

Traditional education goes against the fundamental principle of **discipline**, which is knowing yourself. Knowing yourself requires learning the ability to govern yourself, possessing the aptitude to reflect on the reality of the world, and choosing your own path.

If, from childhood, you're taught standardized things that everyone must learn at the same pace, and your day is structured with different subjects within a limited time, followed by a bell that announces each hour when you need to stop and change classes, all these elements are part of a very carefully designed social engineering to train humans to obey and not give them time to think for themselves.

As I mentioned, great things happen to the human spirit when it is left free. That is precisely what the elite that governs the world doesn't want to happen.

For me, it's very important to explain this point well because I know that many people still think that the best thing about society is precisely its educational system. But as I emphasize in my book *A World of Illusions*, not everything we see is reality.

This doesn't mean the cause is lost and that we can't do anything about it. It's in our hands to change the course of our lives once we detect something that doesn't work for us.

I also don't suggest pulling our children out of the education system immediately, but we must remain alert and see if the education they're receiving in school is really of quality. In the United States, the practice of homeschooling has significantly increased in recent years, especially after the COVID-19 pandemic.

The reasons for this increase are mainly that parents are looking for a more flexible and personalized option for their children, as well as greater control over the content and environment of their education. The idea honestly doesn't seem crazy, considering that before the 17th century, education was mostly given at home.

As far as discipline is concerned, what is certain is that an environment that promotes free will in the choice of what to study and how to study is definitely more enriching than a punitive, inflexible, and impersonal environment. As Professor John Taylor Gatto emphasizes:

> *"Discipline begins with solitude... with the ability to be alone with oneself and reflect, without the need for structured schedules, no agendas, no tasks, no planned free time."*

Chapter 7 | Interpersonal Relationships

"For love, we not only copy the values of our parents, but also their diseases."

—ALEJANDRO JODOROWSKY

Our first social interaction circle is the family. Your family relationships have a significant impact on your personal and emotional development. In fact, the family is the primary source of learning. Our parents are the first people we form an emotional and affectionate bond with, and they also teach us the fundamental principles of discipline.

If you grew up in a disordered or overly rigid environment, both conditions will affect how you relate to discipline. Friends and those close to us also have a major influence on our personal decisions. If you're surrounded by friends who don't support your growth, it can halt the unfolding of your full potential.

Some people confuse discipline with having a rigid life with strict schedules and no flexibility—something like a militarized agenda where we perform tasks like robots. This, however, is not the kind of discipline we are after. While such rigidity may lead to good results, it's unsustainable without an intrinsic goal.

What matters more is developing discipline from within the mind, not simply following rigid instructions with no particular meaning. Mental training requires rigorous control over our thoughts and a meticulous analysis of how these thoughts affect cause and effect—how they impact our perception of others, and how they also change life circumstances by connecting cause and effect. It's about patiently practicing the ability to learn and investigate.

How Family Relationships Influence the Development of Discipline

As the central nucleus of humanity, family relationships are the strongest and most influential bonds throughout our lives. When we are born, we inherit our family's genealogy; as Alejandro Jodorowsky says, "your body knows your parents."

At birth, we are predisposed to the direct influence of our family. We "inherit" genetic traits and influences from our great-grandparents, grandparents, parents, uncles, and siblings. From the moment we are identified with a name, our parents are already shaping the type of person we will become and the achievements we will reach.

From childhood, we are imposed with family ideas and taboos that hinder the potential of our true "self." If our parents led mediocre lives or pursued a specific profession, all their unfulfilled dreams and desires fall upon us at birth. This is the classic example of a father who always dreamed his son would become a football player, doctor, or lawyer. He is projecting his frustration and transferring his expectations to his child, who now bears that burden and feels pressured to meet those expectations.

Or the mother who always wanted to be a ballet dancer and, upon having a daughter, pushes her into ballet classes—even against the girl's will—when the child may actually have been inclined toward art or painting.

Why is it important to recognize this? Because the family element is one of the deepest pillars, and a key piece to understanding why, as adults, we feel frustrated with our own decisions. We often don't realize that the choices we think we made "on our own" were actually made unconsciously—without questioning whether they are authentic, whether they stem from the depths of our being, or if we were simply influenced by our parents' pressures.

The premise of this book is based on the idea that discipline, far from being a rigid and inflexible mechanism that makes you act automatically—like training a dog to sit or obey its owner—is actually the ability to raise our consciousness and unleash the creative force of the "Self." This operates on the level of awareness that allows us to act in alignment with our deepest desires.

That's why it's crucial to detect and become aware of how much our family has influenced our decisions, lifestyle, and how this continues to impact (negatively or perhaps positively) the pursuit of our goals.

"Everyone should know their family tree. The family is either our treasure chest or our death trap."

—ALEJANDRO JODOROWSKY

Your Friends Are Not Always Your Allies

Social pressure and influence can jeopardize your ability to develop good discipline. Just like our family, friends and partners exert a huge influence on how we live our lives. There's a popular saying that goes, "If you want to see a reflection of your life, look at the five people closest to you."

It's true that we tend to surround ourselves with people who think similarly or lead a lifestyle similar to ours. In most cases, our best friends are made during childhood, at school or in the neighborhood where we grew up.

As we grow, we increasingly depend on social approval from our peers. Canadian psychologist Gordon Neufeld and clinical doctor Gabor Maté, in their book *Hold On to Your Kids: Why Parents Need to Matter More Than Kids*, argue that when children suffer emotional neglect at home, they tend to develop a dangerous psychological dependence on their schoolmates. They seek the social approval and attention they didn't receive at home.

In our adolescence, we still lack the maturity to consciously choose our friendships. Under the pressure to "be cool," we tend to want to belong to groups that—also trying to fill a void—engage in behaviors meant to "impress" others, such as drinking alcohol, breaking rules, having sex with multiple partners, smoking, using drugs, bullying others, and other typical adolescent behaviors. This is how we experience our teenage years: imitating idols, challenging our parents, and feeling disconnected from an authentic "self."

Finally, in adulthood, we live by comparing ourselves to others in an endless race to see who has more: we compare our homes, cars, achievements, clothes, careers, partners, families... Life becomes a race, a meaningless competition for objects or status, which, in the best case, are fleeting, and in the worst, nonexistent.

Our circle of friends is our refuge for social approval. It's a way of feeling integrated into a world we don't fully understand. Being accepted by a social group becomes a survival mechanism, a comfort zone.

But what happens when you want more than just to belong to that social group and begin to stand out? Your friends are the first to notice. You start to feel that their conversations about trivial matters and the gossip of the moment no longer interest you as they once did. When you start succeeding, some may even try to downplay your achievements with hurtful comments or disbelief. It bothers them that someone who was "just like them" can excel while they remain stagnant.

I'm sure that on more than one occasion, you've expressed your desire to change your life situation, to do something new—perhaps leave your toxic job for one that aligns better with your values. Surely, more than one person has tried to "burst your bubble" with a discouraging comment. For instance, there's always the colleague who will say, " Mate,I don't think it's a good idea to quit your stable job. With the economy like it is, it's not easy to make a living, especially if you have a family to support... and look at the unemployment rates," offering a list of supposed reasons why it's not a good idea to change careers.

Or the well-meaning friend who, when you share your goal of losing weight, says something that discourages you or makes you question your own intention: "Darling, I don't know why you want to lose weight; you look great as you are," or "Being curvy is in fashion now," or "Enjoy life and enjoy food," and so on. These comments may discourage you, but you think they're well-intentioned advice. In most cases, they are, because your friends are still in that state of mind where they don't see any advantage in stepping out of their comfort zones.

Others might say these things as a defense mechanism because your desire to succeed and your achievements threaten their status quo. Your success exposes them to their own mediocrity.

Unfortunately, we live in a world filled with insecure and envious people. Some of them may even be our family members or closest friends. They fear failure, and they also fear your success. When we transcend what we once thought was impossible, push our limits, and become more, our light reflects on the walls they've built for themselves. In other words, your light makes them see the barriers of their own prison.

Surround yourself with friends who support your decisions. The number of friends truly willing to support you may not be as high as you'd expect, but as Jim Morrison once said, "A true friend is one who gives you the freedom to be yourself."

As you become the person you truly want to be, you will lose friendships you once thought valued you, but that drift away as they see you changing. Along the way, you'll meet new people who align with your new lifestyle and values.

A PERSON DOES NOT ATTRACT WHAT THEY WANT, BUT WHAT THEY ARE.

If you want to know who you are, look at the five people closest to you. This will reveal valuable information to help you assess whether you're on the right path or need to make a change.

Make friends who want the best for you. As the famous psychologist Jordan Peterson says, "Friendships are a reciprocal arrangement. You're not morally obligated to support someone who is making the world a worse place. On the contrary, you should choose people who want the best for you."

Be Careful Who You Choose as a Life Partner

Your partner can either be your salvation or your burden. A partner who doesn't respect your aspirations can lead to failure, anxiety, and even depression. The prominent psychologist

Abraham Maslow clearly states: "A musician must make music, a painter must paint, a poet must write, if you want to be happy in the end. What a person can be, they must be. This is what we call self-actualization."

Why should the love you feel for your partner require you to abandon your personal aspirations for fulfillment? If your partner doesn't support your life goals and doesn't back your decisions, you must reconsider whether it's worth staying in that relationship.

Maybe your partner is afraid of your success. They might feel threatened, thinking that your success could "overshadow" their own existence. Or they may even think they deserve to be the "successful" one more than you do.

These situations can be very hard to detect. In the beginning, they often manifest as subtle, manipulative comments such as, "You spend more time practicing your music than with me," or "You care more about your work than about me."

Such comments are already a sign that your partner may have an issue with you investing time in your projects. I know it's not easy to notice when you're in this situation. After all, when you commit to a person, there's an expectation of building a shared life project. That project should be fulfilling for both, helping both partners grow and self-actualize.

If your partner asks you to sacrifice your dreams for the sake of the relationship, the relationship is unhealthy. If, in order to make the person you love happy, you have to give up who you are and your aspirations, and force yourself to fit into the "person" your partner expects you to be, then the line between healthy love and manipulation, dependence, or even passive violence has been crossed.

Let's remember the wise words of Immanuel Kant, who reminds us that humanity itself is worthy, and that humans should be treated as ends in themselves, not as means to an end. As the psychologist and author Walter Riso affirms:

"It doesn't matter how much they love you, but how they love you. It's a matter of total quality."

Society is a Mental Prison

From the moment we are born, society begins to exert its influence on our thoughts, habits, and actions to make us "fit in." What does it mean to fit into society? Simply put, it means becoming just another number, a reflection of the social group we are born into. Going to school, working, paying taxes, consuming, staying within conventional molds, not standing out, eating the same things, dressing similarly, going to the same places, aspiring to the same things.

The influence of society is so powerful for some people that it creates a genuine fear of not fitting in. In the place where I was born, "belonging" to the local society was of great importance and even seen as an achievement, like when you "rose" from a humble social circle to one with greater resources.

Every place we are born has its cultural roots, which we begin to learn from an early age. Many people develop personalities that fiercely defend the cultural identity they belong to, without questioning whether the values they promote are sexist, racist, cruel, or unjust.

In Monterrey, my hometown in Mexico, it is a source of great pride to eat *carne asada* (Grilling) every weekend. It's also common to use expressions like "*güey*," (dude) "*qué padre*,"(how cool) "*está fregón*," (awesome) and so on. Having the "*regio*" accent is a must; otherwise, people will consider you an "outsider." There are only two football teams: you are either a *Tigre* or a *Rayado*. If you prefer another team, you're considered strange or, again, an "outsider."

Don't know who *Bronco* is? Outsider! Boxes, boxes, all made the same. One is pink, the other is green… but in the end, they are all boxes, all made the same way.

Societies are like these circles of repetition, where every citizen must follow a predetermined role: they must obey the rules, speak the language, inherit the customs and traditions to "be part of the clan."

I won't deny that it feels good to be part of a social group, to feel that you belong somewhere.

I know exactly what I'm talking about because I experienced it firsthand when I moved to Switzerland, where my "*regio*"accent, being a fan of the *Rayados*, and my love for *carne asada* were of no use. That's when I felt the existential void of "not belonging."

Of course, I tried to fit into the "Swiss box." I tried to understand their customs, learn their Swiss-German dialect (fifteen years and counting…), adopt their habits, like putting out the trash at the designated time and with the right-colored bag to avoid being fined… and yes, becoming a fan of raclette cheese.

My frustration with trying to fit into the "Swiss box" and my total failure to do so almost led me into a depressive nostalgia. I wanted to shape "the Swiss box" into a more Mexican form. I failed because it's like trying to use raclette cheese in a red enchilada. Practically incomprehensible.

We can become so trapped by our "cultures" that our true identity suffers outside of social definitions. Who am I? Am I Mexican? Am I Swiss? I'm human. My home is where my heart is. My culture is the culture of the world.

I freed myself when I realized that I don't have to fit into any box, that the human soul is vast and contains everything. Why should I worry about fitting into a box when I don't need to be inside one? It's a **liberating** feeling.

Challenging the limits of your box becomes a life mission. Every individual is ultimately the result of two forces: the imitative force (reinforced by the family, social, and cultural group) and the creative force (the consciousness that is you, the unique spark of your own divinity).

We are all subject to those invisible forces of imitation: beliefs, habits, traditions, and restrictions. When you become aware, you can access the creative force, which projects itself toward pure universal consciousness, the origin of Creation. By transcending this reality, you discover your true creative "Self." You break the spell and enter into reality.

"The ultimate goal of discipline is to free the creative force of the Self."

—RAIMON SAMSÓ

Chapter 8 | Fear

"Fear is Your Prison."
—PAOLA KNECHT

Undoubtedly, fear is another root of mental imprisonment. The fear of dying, but more specifically, the fear of living. In the reality we live in, we are programmed to "accept" fear as a normal human feeling.

Yes, of course, no one wants to die. Nobody in their right mind wants to die. It's so paradoxical that the fear of death consumes people to the point that they would literally rather "not live." And I'm not referring to cases of suicidal people, but rather to the fear of death itself, where people prefer to stay trapped in their small mental box.

This mental box looks something like this: society demands that you take on a productive role. You go to school to please your parents, and therefore, to follow societal norms. You obey authority because you think that if you don't, you'll face unpleasant consequences.

You spend your whole life seeking social approval, belonging to the status quo, following everything others say. You have respect for people called "experts" in all sorts of areas: health, education, well-being, lifestyle, what's good and what's not... in short, you never have time to develop your own opinions or find **your own voice.**

You follow government and societal mandates, fear losing your job, and not being able to provide for your family. You feel incapable of generating your own wealth because you were taught all your life that you need to be an employee and that "there are not enough resources for everyone."

You're afraid to express your desires and authenticity for fear of being criticized or kicked out of the group. You fear contracting viruses floating around and, based on what "health authorities" recommend or, in some countries, even require you to do—like getting vaccinated or taking dubious medications (for more details, see my book *A World of Illusions*).

In the world of fear, there is no personal sovereignty; we are puppets following invisible orders. We are like the donkey running in circles, trying to reach the carrot without realizing it's tied to our own tail.

It's the "mini me," which has no power, a victim of the harsh world.

Fear is the ultimate prison—it's the energy that has us completely dominated as a human species. Perhaps you've noticed that I keep saying we are "dominated" and "manipulated." And yes, it's literally true.

There are human and non-human powers that control human reality perception. Fear is a low-vibration energy that is used to manipulate and control, but we must understand the whole territory because knowledge is power.

When you become aware that all "fear" is a vibrational energy that only affects you when you identify with it, then you hold the liberating key... the key to the doors of **freedom.**

As David Icke says in his book *The Answer*: "If you believe in the 'mini me, I have no power' concept, you will live a life that expresses that identity, as your perceptual state is transmitted in waves that intertwine and synchronize with one another."

What the brilliant Icke means in practical terms is that by thinking you're a loser, undeserving of success, happiness, love, and abundance, you'll attract people, situations, and experiences into your life that reflect that mental state... which ends up becoming a self-fulfilling prophecy.

If you want to control someone at all costs, what mechanism do you use to make that person obey and do what you want? *Voilà*! You manipulate them through fear. My friend, it's time to break free from the prison.

Part Two | Reprogram your mind

"Every man is where he is by the law of his being; the thoughts which he has built into his character have brought him there, and in the arrangement of his life, there is no element of chance, but all is the result of a law which cannot err."

—JAMES ALLEN

Everything begins with the mind. The way we discipline our mind determines the quality of our life. An undisciplined, chaotic mind leads to an equally chaotic life. This is a law of nature, immutable and integral to the human experience.

Disciplining the mind, however, is far from easy. If it were, we wouldn't need psychologists, self-help books, yoga practices, or the endless stream of expert advice flooding YouTube and Instagram about mental health, balance, and the elusive quest for peace and prosperity.

So why is it so hard to control our minds? What dark forces conspire to keep us perpetually distracted, overwhelmed, and exhausted? Personally, I believe there are indeed shadowy forces at play, as I've mentioned in earlier chapters. Modern society is designed for everything but **peace of mind**.

This relentless frenzy has left us chronically unwell. We crave instant gratification and try to bypass life's natural processes. But here's the good news: not all is lost. The first step toward healing and regaining control of our mind is recognizing that we're battling an invisible enemy. And this enemy is closer than you think—it's part of you. It operates in your conscious and subconscious mind, shaping your perception of reality.

Our consciousness doesn't have to be our foe; in fact, it's our greatest ally against chaos. You may wonder: how do we transform it into our friend?

Once we acknowledge and confront this inner adversary, the rest isn't as daunting as it might seem. It's often said that practice makes perfect, and cultivating self-discipline demands more than good intentions and the desire to change.

How often have we set out with the best intentions, only to abandon our goals along the way? I know this struggle all too well. One of the greatest challenges of the 21st century is our diminished ability to focus and concentrate on achieving seemingly "difficult" goals.

In the early 20th century, society redefined the nature of work. The industrial era introduced automation, standardizing tasks and creating repetitive, assembly-line jobs. The aim was clear: eventually replace human labor with machines.

This dehumanization of work also impacted our understanding of discipline. It stripped away curiosity and the joy of effort, reducing it to a mechanical routine.

When discipline becomes an obligation driven by pressure, fear, or external expectations, the results are predictable. You may sustain the effort briefly, but long-term persistence without an inner spark is unsustainable.

True discipline endures only when it arises from the depths of our psyche—from either our primal instincts or higher consciousness.

A vivid example of this can be seen in a child learning to walk. That inner drive, nestled within their small frame, propels them to try again and again until they succeed. The same applies when they learn to ride a bike, eat with utensils, or dress themselves. The process is slow but inevitable. It's an intrinsic part of being human.

Before we dive into the most effective methods for calming and disciplining the mind, let's first explore some foundational concepts for cultivating healthy discipline.

Chapter 9 | The Power of Self-Awareness

There's a famous saying: "*Good thoughts can only bring good results. Bad thoughts can never produce good results.*"Self-discipline is the greatest gift you can give yourself.

To embark on the journey of discipline, we must start with the basics, which means addressing a fundamental question:

What is DISCIPLINE?

GENERALLY, DISCIPLINE TENDS TO HAVE A BAD REPUTATION. It's often perceived as a series of rigid, mechanical habits that stifle creative thought. But in reality, it's quite the opposite.

The word *discipline* comes from the Latin term *discipulus*, meaning "student" or "follower." In Latin, *discipulus* also refers to "instruction" and "knowledge." Therefore, self-discipline means being both your own student and your own follower. In essence, discipline is about "following your own Master," which—yes, you guessed it—comes from within you!

At its core, discipline is an act of self-love, an inherent state of consciousness that exists within us but often goes unnoticed. It's there, ready to support us, the moment we make that deeply personal decision to embrace it.

Many books and podcasts feature psychologists and experts who argue that discipline is not a universal trait we're all born with. Personally, I disagree. From my personal and professional experience, I've observed that every individual possesses the innate capacity for discipline and can activate it at any time. It's simply a matter of making a conscious choice.

The problem lies in our inability to recognize this quality as part of our very nature. Humanity has thrived throughout history because of its struggle, its burning desire to survive and succeed.

To achieve everything we have as a civilization, there had to be a force within both our individual and collective consciousness. This force not only motivated us to survive but also propelled us to transcend survival and reach an advanced state of being.

This is why I believe discipline is an act of self-love. It's about making a commitment to your personal growth, proving to yourself that the life you want is achievable because you love yourself enough to fight for it.

Above all, it's also a commitment to God. We draw closer to God when we accept and respect His divine design—our mind and body. There's a passage in the Bible that says, *"Do to others as you would have them do to you"* (Luke 6:31), and another that states, *"Love your neighbor as yourself"* (Matthew 22:36). Reading these together invites us to reflect on how we view ourselves.

Most of the time, we're more committed to meeting others' demands than fulfilling our own. Discipline, at its simplest, is about honoring the self.

Self-Esteem Is Your Best Ally

Many people confuse self-love with selfishness, but they are fundamentally different. Selfishness is thinking only of oneself, often at the expense of others, and is rooted in fear—fear of losing attention, resources, power, or influence.

Self-esteem, on the other hand, stems from love—for life and existence itself. It's about recognizing your divine origin and admiring creation and existence. When you look in the mirror, you're not just seeing a person; you're seeing the reflection of limitless potential.

Loving yourself is a divine commandment. While this might sound like a cliché or superficial sentiment, there's scientific reasoning behind it.

Our body functions optimally only when we're in complete balance. Both mental and sensory functions operate at their best when we're healthy and happy. An imbalanced body—whether due to stress or poor diet—tends to fall ill. Illness, at its core, is a lack of energy. And where does energy come from?

Your entire conscious universe is energy. Your body and mind are energy capsules vibrating at different frequencies. When your body resonates in harmony with the surrounding energy field, you experience well-being on the "earthly plane." This harmony originates from consciousness—what we call the mind.

Psychologist Keith Floyd puts it succinctly: *"Contrary to popular belief, consciousness does not arise from the brain. Rather, consciousness creates the appearance of the brain."*

Love is the creative energy of the universe. What we call "love" is a state of consciousness vibrating at an extraordinarily high frequency. This frequency is the birthplace of creation. True self-love means aligning yourself with this creative force of the universe.

This is why the Bible emphasizes: *"Love your neighbor as*

yourself" (Matthew 22:36), *"Love the Lord your God with all your heart"* (Mark 12:30), and *"God created man in His own image"* (Genesis 1:26).

Metaphorically, Christ's teachings suggest that loving yourself is loving existence itself. According to the laws of Creation and nature, a body in harmony aligns perfectly with the vibrational energy of the universe.

I use Biblical passages to illustrate this truth, but I'm not referring to God as a humanoid figure to adore. Rather, I see God as an infinite source of energy—the very power of Creation. We are part of that power, which means we are creators of reality.

Chapter 10 | Determination

Determination is the blend of passion and perseverance—a quality that pushes you forward despite obstacles. It is a trait that reveals itself through the character of an individual. According to Robert Greene in *The Laws of Human Nature*, one key indicator of character is the consistency of actions over time.

While people often claim they've learned their lessons, the true indicator of their character lies in the decisions they make throughout their lives. No one does something "just once." If we observe carefully, most actions follow a defined and often compulsive pattern.

For instance, if someone promises to deliver a project on time or arrive early to a meeting but fails to follow through, it's likely a recurring compulsive behavior they may not even be aware of. To develop unshakable discipline, we must pay close attention to our own compulsive actions. Are there patterns in how we decide and act?

In a mentoring session, a client shared that he felt uncomfortable with his weight but found it "impossible" to make time for exercise. He had to leave early for work, and by evening, he was too exhausted to get off the couch.

When we reviewed the decisions he'd made in various areas of his life over the past few years, we uncovered a compulsive pattern: he consistently postponed tasks he perceived as "less gratifying." This behavior extended beyond fitness and affected other aspects of his life as well.

For example, his lack of energy and motivation made it hard to imagine waking up earlier for exercise. He spent most of his day sitting at a desk and his evenings lounging on the couch, which reinforced his sedentary habits. His eating patterns further exacerbated the problem—he consumed high-carb foods to counter his low energy, leading to blood sugar spikes and a persistent sense of fatigue.

Additionally, he realized much of his day was spent in tension and stress. The demands of his job exceeded what he could reasonably handle. Overeating and binge-watching Netflix became easy escapes from confronting the deeper issue: dissatisfaction with his work.

Once he identified the root cause, he was able to replace it with a stronger purpose. What started as a request for help with weight loss evolved into a broader plan to address his career dissatisfaction and its impact on his lifestyle.

By carefully observing his actions and committing to change the habits that didn't align with his goals, he began transforming his reality.

His initial goal to exercise more—combined with objectives like improving his health, increasing energy levels, reducing anxiety and stress, and achieving balance—led him to take consistent positive actions toward better health. Over time, these efforts resulted in significant weight loss and improved overall well-being.

Once we set the right goals, **determination** becomes our

greatest ally in persevering. The key to success lies in maintaining sustained focus in a specific direction long enough to see results.

Redefining Failure

The phrase *"I don't have failures; I've just learned how not to do things"* is a cliché we've all heard. However, its vital role in reshaping our mindset and improving our lives is often overlooked.

Failure is uncomfortable—it hurts. Most people struggle to handle failure in a healthy way. Instead, they feel depressed, give up, or become indifferent. For many, failure leads to abandoning their dreams prematurely.

To cultivate strong discipline, we must systematically address our relationship with failure. It's essential to detach negative emotions from actions labeled as "failures." Instead, we must see failure as a checkpoint for evaluation and recalibration, which is its true purpose.

The feeling of failure often stems from a belief that "others are watching." Even if no one notices your failure, you might magnify the event in your mind, creating the illusion that the whole world is judging you.

By changing how we interpret and respond to failure, we can transform it into a tool for growth. Here are some ways to shift perspective:

- **View failure as a teacher**, offering valuable lessons.
- **See it as an opportunity** to gain wisdom and insight.
- **Recognize failure as a natural part of life's process**, necessary for progress.

- **Turn failure into perseverance and determination**, treating it as just one more step.

"Failure is simply the opportunity to begin again, this time more intelligently."
— HENRY FORD

Chapter 11 | A Resilient Mind

Resilience is one of the most fascinating traits of the human mind. It has roots in our most ancient past and, to some extent, remains a mystery. Our bodies, operating in dimensions beyond our conscious intervention, already possess the perfect mechanisms for resilience.

The human body has demonstrated extraordinary resilience over time, adapting to extreme environments. Humans thrive in some of the coldest places on Earth, like Siberia, where temperatures plummet to -68°C, and in the hottest, such as the deserts of Iran, where temperatures soar to 70°C.

Since everything originates in consciousness, I believe that mental resilience—defined as "the ability to adapt to and overcome life's challenges"—is also something we can consciously access. In my view, we don't need to wait for resilience to develop over time as we're often told. Instead, we can actively summon it when needed.

A common example of resilience is adapting to a new country and culture. Initially, based on your habits and beliefs, understanding and accepting a different way of life can be challenging.

However, the real obstacle often lies not in the culture itself but in how we perceive, think about, and judge our new environment.

When someone says, "I can't adapt to the culture," they often mean, "I don't understand it," or even, "I don't like it" or "I'm not interested in adapting." Without a conscious decision to adapt, we remain at the surface, thinking, "I'll adapt over time," which is often an excuse for postponing the effort.

Research into resilience often highlights the brain's ability to rewire itself, a phenomenon known as **neuroplasticity.** According to this theory, adapting to a new culture is just a matter of time as your brain forms new connections. However, if years pass without adaptation, it raises a crucial question: does time alone foster resilience, or is it a matter of shifting how we perceive challenges?

For years, I believed resilience was like a muscle that required training. Facing unpleasant situations repeatedly would, over time, build strength through neuroplasticity. While technically true, this understanding only scratched the surface.

Why are some people naturally more resilient than others?

Why do some individuals overcome severe trauma while others never recover?

Why do renowned artists or athletes, after reaching the pinnacle of success, spiral into depression or destructive habits?

If neuroplasticity were the sole answer, wouldn't their years of rigorous training have given them unshakable mental strength?

The truth goes deeper. **The subconscious mind governs much of our lives.** Training the rational mind to demand the unimaginable and embrace new paradigms is essential. Resilience is not merely a repetitive practice but a conscious decision.

A resilient mind is a decisive mind. A clear and firm decision sends a powerful command to the subconscious, which then acts accordingly.

Embracing Flexibility

In a world where the only constant is change, flexibility becomes a vital trait. Who you were a moment ago is no longer who you are now. We live in a perpetual present where the past and future continuously evolve.

Even as you read this, the words you just finished are now part of the past, and the moment I wrote them was my present, which for you exists in the future.

Time, as we understand it, is a human construct to measure existence. Nothing is static; everything evolves and is alive at every moment. Flexibility doesn't mean abandoning discipline, plans, or structure. Instead, it involves adapting to new circumstances rather than resisting them.

We are the creators of our own reality. Every moment contributes to shaping your immediate present and future. Discipline, in this sense, is about maintaining focus on thoughts, actions, and states of consciousness that bring fulfillment.

> "With discipline, it's not about being the best;
> it's about being better than yesterday."
> – PAOLA KNECHT

Chapter 12 | Staying Alert

Focusing on daily tasks is crucial, but we must not forget the importance of staying alert to what's happening around us. Sometimes, we believe our daily actions are helping us achieve our goals, but when we take a closer look at the actual results, we may find that those actions are no longer relevant to our current circumstances.

Maintaining a curious and open mind is essential for cultivating strong discipline. By consistently questioning the *why* behind things, your mind remains active and ready to adopt new habits and beliefs that align with your personal growth.

When we are born, we are pure, infinite consciousness—without any restrictions. However, even from that early stage, societal, cultural, and familial "cages" begin to enclose us. These cages limit our thoughts, trapping us in societal norms we often refer to as "civilized behavior." It's no wonder that at some point, despite doing everything "right," we feel utterly lost.

This happened to me. Early in my career, I strictly followed the societal blueprint:

- Study hard.
- Get good grades.
- Pursue internships.
- Work at multinational companies to gain experience.
- Climb the corporate ladder.

My ambition to "do things right" led me to believe that I had to abide by these rules. I graduated with honors in engineering, earned an executive master's degree, and began working for global companies. I felt on top of my game... until, suddenly, something inside me began to crumble.

There came a time when getting out of bed each morning felt like a monumental task. Mondays became unbearable. By Sunday night, anxiety gripped me as I braced for the dreaded start of the workweek. Like Garfield, I adopted the mantra, *"I Hate Mondays."*

The idea of endless to-do lists, impossible projects, toxic people, and the bureaucracy of corporate life filled me with dread.

Eventually, I lost the motivation to keep climbing the corporate ladder. I felt ashamed and guilty for being exhausted by a world I had built with my own choices. Without motivation, focusing on doing my job well became a struggle, and I couldn't find meaning in my work.

To maintain my reputation, I forced myself to keep going—to give it my all. But like an overworked machine, I finally collapsed. I realized that the path I once thought ideal for my life and success was no longer serving me. If I didn't change course urgently, I would push myself into complete burnout.

I decided to invest more time in activities that truly ignited my passion but with a professional focus. I began writing and publishing books. I pursued professional certifications to develop the skills needed to provide coaching and mentorship. I devoted myself to reading and studying topics that sparked joy within me.

Waking up at 5 or 6 in the morning became a delight when I knew the day ahead would be filled with writing, helping others, and spending time with my family. These activities filled me with such purpose that I no longer struggled to get out of bed. In fact, I now go to sleep feeling deeply satisfied, knowing that another day of doing what I love awaits.

As Alejandro Jodorowsky wisely said, "The intellect proposes; intuition realizes." Pay close attention to what your intellect suggests versus what your intuition tells you. When in doubt, always—**always**—choose intuition. It is infinitely more powerful than the intellect. Try it, and you'll see.

Steve Jobs was also an advocate for staying tuned to intuition, stating:

"Intuition is a very powerful thing, more powerful than intellect, in my opinion. It has had a tremendous impact on my work."

Stay alert. Stay curious. Trust yourself.

Chapter 13 | Motivation

You've probably experienced this: once you set a goal—whether it's losing weight, buying a house, changing professions, or achieving a job promotion—when the idea forms in your mind, you feel energized and ready to act. You start making a list of everything you need to do to tackle the objective: you go to the supermarket and buy nutritious foods, sign up for the gym, enroll in courses, and so on. Initially, you're brimming with enthusiasm, feeling just a step away from achieving it.

But after a few days or weeks, you realize you haven't lost any weight, face difficulties at work, and start feeling discouraged. By the time you get home, sitting on the couch to watch a Netflix series becomes more tempting than going out to exercise or hitting the gym. The vegetables you bought for smoothies and healthy salads end up rotting in the fridge. After all, it takes time and energy to chop vegetables and make a salad... better to have some pasta or order a pizza; it's more satisfying and requires less effort, right?

The harsh reality is that if we wait to feel motivated to do something, we'll never get anywhere. Why? Because motivation is an emotion that doesn't occur consistently. Many factors can determine whether you feel motivated: lack of sleep, a bad experience with someone, if you're sick... and the list goes on. If we rely solely on motivation to achieve a goal, the likelihood of giving up is quite high.

This is precisely why it's essential to train the mind to act "despite..." For example, you want to jog every morning, but on the first day you plan to start, it rains... do it despite the rain! Jogging in the rain can be wonderful and refreshing.

You want to start a diet but wake up tired and with strong cravings for something sweet? Make yourself a vegetable juice, stick to the diet even if you don't feel like it. Ignore the feeling and act. Determination to achieve something is what will, over time, become your best ally in accomplishing your goals.

In fact, I'm convinced that action itself generates the motivation to keep pursuing our objectives, not the other way around as is commonly believed. I've seen many cases of people who started working towards a goal without much initial motivation, but after maintaining consistency in their actions for some time, they began to see results, which then ignited the motivation to continue.

All life's processes follow a particular order to manifest successfully. In the case of discipline, I propose starting with determination (instead of motivation).

Determination involves having a firm purpose, a clear vision of what you want to achieve. In this context, the "What" is more important than the "How." If you worry about the "How" without having a clear understanding of the "What," the probability of achieving something is minimal.

I believe that the vast majority of people who suffer from Impostor Syndrome do so precisely because they weren't clear about what they wanted to achieve from the beginning. They start with a very general idea and end up getting lost in the "How."

"I want to make more money." Okay, but "How am I going to achieve that?"

The "How" can get lost in the infinite; there are a thousand ways to make money... but if you don't know exactly how much you want and what that money truly represents to you, then taking action becomes quite difficult. This naturally leads us to formulate our vision.

Chapter 14 | Vision

Continuing with the example from the previous chapter, there is a significant difference between saying, "I want to earn more money" and "I want to earn $10,000 per month." The second statement is much clearer and more comprehensible for the subconscious mind, which plays a crucial role in manifesting desires into material reality.

For the subconscious, "Earn more money" could mean $1, $5, $100, or $100,000 more—it could mean anything or nothing. Without a precise instruction, this ambiguity leads to inaction. A vague goal like "earn more money" becomes an unattainable wish, lacking the passion and intrinsic determination necessary to sustain effort and consistency. "Achieve what?" the subconscious wonders.

Most personal development books emphasize visualization as a tool for manifesting reality: "Visualize your dream house, the money you need, those vacations to exotic destinations, the lifestyle you desire." While this sounds appealing, visualization alone does not work magic.

Everyone dreams of living in a mansion, traveling to fascinating places, earning more money, working less, and enjoying life more. However, very few people invest enough time and effort to define precisely what they want to achieve and create a clear, compelling vision for it.

Having worked extensively in the corporate world, I've noticed a similar pattern even in large organizations. For instance, it's not enough for a company to state, "We want to be a global leader." Leader of what? What exactly will you offer your customers? What value will they gain from your product or service? How much must you sell or earn to qualify as a "global leader"?

So, we recognize the importance of having a vision. But what if you don't know what your vision is?

In my book *The Success Mindset,* I present a simple yet powerful method to help you craft more concrete visions for any area of your life. Here's a summary of the steps:

1. Discover what you love to do.
2. Identify what you're good at.
3. Determine what truly excites you.
4. Define your vocation.
5. Formulate your mission.
6. Combine all the above into a single statement that encapsulates the legacy you wish to leave in the world —this becomes your vision.

When we have a clear vision of what we want to achieve, the likelihood of success becomes far greater than if our minds have no concrete image to work toward.

In his remarkable book *Feeling is the Secret,* Neville Goddard explains how human beings control creation through the power of imagination, combined with emotion and the deliberate selection of ideas they hold in their minds.

The clearer and more dominant this idea is in your mind, the stronger the resulting action will be—action that eventually manifests your desire in the *"external world."*

Maintain a clear, consistent vision of what you genuinely want to achieve over time, and you will see results.

"Circumstances do not make the man; they reveal him to himself."

—JAMES ALLEN, *As a Man Thinketh*

Chapter 15 | Focus

You've probably heard the phrase, *"You are what you think."* But is this truly the case? By now, I hope you're at least considering it seriously. Still, it's not just our thoughts that define us but also our feelings, which originate from bioenergetic processes.

Everything is energy, and energy represents the information transmitted and processed by the brain. The brain deciphers and distorts the hyper-complex field of vast information contained in the **Lattice**, or what we often refer to as the "void."*

What does this mean? Essentially, our consciousness selects the information the brain decodes and transmits, which then projects onto our three-dimensional perception of reality.

Of course, much of the information—or "programs"—processed by the brain operates outside our conscious awareness. From birth, we inherit certain types of information, such as:

---

* Jacobo Grinberg-Zylberbaum: The Syntergic Theory, Instituto Nacional para el Estudio de la Conciencia, 1990

- Genetic coding from our family,
- The environmental context of the society or country we are born into,
- The collective consciousness of humanity itself.

Our spark of consciousness, which begins pure and pristine at birth, is quickly influenced as it interacts with other vibrational frequencies of information.

Consider for a moment that your body—and by extension, your being—functions like a set of powerful information algorithms. These algorithms grow and strengthen based on the data they're fed.

In today's world, much is said about artificial intelligence (AI) and its remarkable ability to learn and process knowledge at astonishing speeds. Feed an algorithm specific information over time, and it starts to learn by forming connections, generating new threads of information, and reinforcing itself. These processes make the algorithm increasingly powerful.

Similarly, your body operates as an extraordinary machine, equipped with advanced algorithms functioning across multiple levels of consciousness. These allow for incredible capacities—cognitive, auditory, visual, and sensory.

Your consciousness is constantly exposed to the information decoded by the brain, meaning you are actively "creating your own reality." Understanding this highlights the importance of consciously choosing the kind of information you feed into your personal "algorithm"—your body and mind.

Imagine someone who is overweight. They look in the mirror and think, "I am obese." This thought sends a signal to the brain, which processes and reinforces the image of an overweight person. The individual's actions then align with this belief: eating junk food, avoiding exercise, wearing clothes that accentuate their weight, and behaving in ways that support this self-image. This cycle feeds the algorithm, continuously affirming the thought: "I am obese."

Now imagine if that same person also believes they are poor and unsuccessful. Here, seemingly clichéd ideas ring true:

"You are what you think."

"You create reality through the quality of our thoughts"

Focus plays a critical role in shaping our reality. The act of observation increases coherence, information processing, and interconnectivity within the brain's structure.

- **Greater synergy** in the brain leads to **stronger algorithms**.
- **Stronger algorithms** create a reality that becomes increasingly aligned with the vibrational frequencies shaping your experiences.

By intentionally focusing on constructive, empowering thoughts and feeding your "algorithm" with high-quality information, you can harness this immense power to reshape your reality.

Chapter 16 | Silence

Spanish writer and poet Pablo d'Ors reminds us in *The Biography of Silence* that at least 80% of our mental activity is irrelevant, or even counterproductive. We all suffer from having a mind that is constantly engaged in an inner dialogue, which has even earned the nickname "the crazy one in the house." If we don't learn to control it, it ends up controlling us. So, how can we master our mind from erratic thinking? The answer lies in silence.

Silence is our ally when we want to learn how to think with quality. Thinking, like any human activity, should be controlled at will. Overthinking paralyzes us; that's why it is said that we think too much but live too little. We fill our minds with chatter that constantly floods our consciousness. Thoughts, if not controlled, fly around like birds fluttering aimlessly in our minds without any sense or direction.

Human beings are accustomed to entertaining themselves with all kinds of experiences, always seeking to fill the void that silence represents. We want to keep the mind occupied in our waking hours: consuming news, gossip, watching TV shows, listening to the opinions of "experts" on all kinds of topics, or checking the latest posts from influencers on Twitter or Instagram.

What do we do with all this information? Where does all that energy go? In the best-case scenario, we ignore it and continue with our daily activities without a problem. But more commonly, we feel overwhelmed and allow ourselves to be carried away by everything we hear. Watching the news today feels like condemning ourselves to a constant state of worry about the world's condition: endless wars, economic crises, natural disasters... News outlets worldwide constantly remind us of the kind of reality we live in: a chaotic, unpredictable, dangerous world full of obstacles. It's no surprise that after watching the news, we lack the positive energy to start the day and pursue our goals.

That's why we need to make a radical change in how we've been taught to live. We must take control of everything that floods our minds, and the best ally to achieve this is connecting with silence. There are different ways to do this, but one that has helped me a lot is practicing **conscious meditation.**

Meditation is a very simple practice, yet many people consider it unproductive. At the end of the day, meditation simply consists of sitting, closing your eyes, focusing on your breath, and becoming aware of the torrent of thoughts. It requires patience and intention. I know there are more interesting activities, like checking social media or planning your next vacation on the beach. Few people recognize the true value of meditation and how this practice transforms the brain.

Numerous studies have shown that meditation has transformative positive effects on our brains. For example, a study by Lazar et al. (2005) found that meditation is linked to an increase in gray matter in brain areas associated with emotional regulation, learning, and memory. Regular meditation increases the thickness of the hippocampus cortex, which is part of the brain's temporal lobe. Dr. Caroline Leaf also argues that directed rest, or keeping the mind calm and directing our rest with introspection and self-reflection, allows for intellectual development, improving the quality of our thoughts by enhancing neural connections (DMN)*, benefiting our mental, spiritual, and physical health.

When we enter directed rest, in other words, a meditative state, we improve the efficiency of unconscious activity. A study by Tang et al. (2007) and Luders et al. (2011) showed that long-term meditation is associated with an increase in interconnectivity between brain regions, particularly those related to attention and concentration. On the other hand, meditation also reduces stress and anxiety by decreasing brain activity in the amygdala, which regulates emotional states like fear. Hözel et al. (2010) found that sustained meditation for eight weeks consecutively reduces activity in the amygdala.

Even though we know about the wonderful benefits of meditation, we live most of our lives outside ourselves, distracted by external events. Meditation is a tool that brings us back home and teaches us to live with our being. Through silence, it is the only way we can observe ourselves without haste, focusing on every detail of our thoughts.

With meditation, we expose ourselves to our true self. Observing our thoughts from our "witness" self is wonderful because it invites us to see our thoughts impersonally. Eventually, if practiced regularly, the mind calms down. You start to see less activity in the torrent of thoughts and begin to enjoy simply being. The entire projection of life as we perceive it disappears, and you can feel the vastness of existence.

Ultimately, a disciplined life is a disciplined mind. Learning to keep our mind in states of silence through meditation is itself a significant achievement on the path to absolute peace.

As you can see, everything is connected. Your desire to

---

* DMP: Default Mode Network

develop good discipline to achieve your goals has as its ultimate state the feeling of peace. When we anxiously chase after our dreams, it's because we don't feel at peace with our current state. We feel that something is missing, and we attribute it to money or to some future state of our life or being.

Silence reminds us of something very valuable: surrendering to life. I'm not referring to surrendering in the sense of giving up and letting ourselves be carried away by bad habits and thoughts, but simply letting go, not holding on to energies that block us, but allowing ourselves to be carried by a serene detachment toward higher energies. As Pablo d'Ors says:

> *"That's why I believe that to write, as to live or love, you don't have to hold on but let go, not to retain, but to detach. The key to almost everything is in the magnanimity of letting go. In love, in art, in meditation—at least these three things work like this."*

Chapter 17 | Stabilize Your Emotions

Human beings are convinced (erroneously) that we are logical animals, and therefore, our decisions are coherent and consistent. In reality, the queen of the world, the one who governs all human activity in every culture, is the queen of **emotions.**

One might think that in more serious environments, like in business, people make decisions based on facts and "raw" information, but nothing could be further from the truth. Neuroscientists specializing in decision-making have confirmed through numerous brain studies that emotional parts of the brain—like the amygdala—are highly active during decision-making processes. This means that, in situations where important decisions are made, emotions can easily override rational thought.

I've observed this phenomenon during all my years working in multinational companies. Sometimes, I was amazed at how these companies, which employ hundreds or even thousands of people to build perfectly functioning systems to help scale their business, make decisions through a very limited group of people, who are often the ones who know the least about the real workings of the company.

So, what do they base their risky decisions on if they don't fully understand what's happening? They base them on their "reasoning," which is influenced by the information they receive from their environment and the emotions associated with that information.

For example, if a CEO receives a report from their team showing positive information—whether it's about increased sales, more clients, or a successful campaign—and is then asked to make a decision about an investment that could ensure the company's continued success, the probability of accepting the risk will be much higher than if the information had been negative.

Even if the numbers are false and the reality is different, the executive will only consider as true the reports provided by trusted members of the board. In our daily lives, we can also observe how almost all (if not all) of the decisions we make stem from an emotion.

The bad mood you feel when you wake up because you didn't sleep well?

The clothes you choose to wear that day?

The breakfast you have?

All these decisions, even the smallest ones, like which side of the bed you get up from, stem from an emotion. This is why I think it's important to address this topic.

Taking control of your emotions is controlling 100% of your life.

I truly believe our existence is governed by emotions. Austrian doctor, psychiatrist, and psychoanalyst Wilhelm Reich refers to the emotions of pleasure, longing, anxiety, rage, and sadness—roughly in that order, according to his own words—as the basic emotions of human beings. His theory is very interesting because it challenges conventional science, which suggests that emotions stem from irrational thought processes.

After conducting numerous studies not only with people but also with other living organisms, he concluded that "Just as all emotions and reactions in life arise from and correspond to sensations from organs and expressive movements; just as living organisms form ideas about their surrounding world from the impressions they receive from the expressions of the world around them; in the same way, all emotions, reactions, and ideas of the armored organism are conditioned by its state of mobility and expression."

What Reich means, in short, is that sensations and emotions are the only link between us and the world around us. We know that objects themselves are things we perceive through image and sensory experiences that make us feel something.

From this, we can deduce that each person perceives themselves and the world around them according to their emotions and their way of judging reality. So, all living organisms perceive themselves and their environment through their sensations and emotions. Understanding this is very powerful because it means we truly have the power to control our emotions and, therefore, change our reality.

Normally, we think that our emotions arise as a consequence of "something" happening in the outside world. If someone makes us angry, or if we "lose" something valuable, we always blame the "circumstances out there."

The reality is that the perception through which we judge the event is what causes us to feel sadness or anxiety, not the event itself. It's the classification with which we infiltrate the projection of our reality that "takes control" of what we feel. Once you realize this, you have the ability to correct the perception and change the emotion.

Of course, this requires practice. Since we were very young, we've been trained to see our reality through the collective eyes of the society we were born into.

OUR MENTAL PROGRAMMING HAS ROOTS IN SOCIAL, CULTURAL, FAMILIAL AND ANCESTRAL FACTORS.

Chapter 18 | Powerful Reprogramming Methods

One of the most fascinating discoveries I've made is realizing that we have the ability to control our minds completely. We can observe every thought, and we also have the power to change them, thereby altering our reality.

This certainty changes everything. I spent my entire life thinking it was impossible to control "the madwoman of the house." I lived with a bunch of birds flying over my head, thoughts that had no order or meaning. Another mistake I made was believing everything I thought, giving equal importance to mundane and critical thoughts.

As you can imagine, it was difficult to act in alignment with my desires. My mind was clouded and confused. With such a mind, it is hard to make decisions that positively impact life. The tendency to procrastinate or give up was very high. That's why learning to discipline the mind is essential, and controlling our thoughts becomes the most important task when it comes to developing discipline.

Once we control our thoughts, we control our emotions. Once our emotions are controlled, discipline in a practical form almost becomes automatic. This is all interconnected because if we generate positive and constructive thoughts, our body's biochemical response will trigger positive emotions and sensations. This will lead us to act in the physical world in a way that aligns with our desired outcomes.

According to Mexican neuroscientist and psychologist Jacobo Grinberg-Zylberbaum, it requires great responsibility and sincerity to accept that the "external" events that shape our personal reality are actually the product of an "individual mental continuum," which is intertwined with the mental continuums of other individuals. Understanding this truth makes us stop using victimhood as a tool for procrastination.

LITERALLY, WE ARE CO-CREATORS OF OUR REALITY IN THE PHYSICAL, MENTAL, AND SPIRITUAL DIMENSIONS.

This brings us to the biblical proverb that says, "So God created mankind in his own image" (Genesis 1:27). God, the creator of all things, has given us the power to co-create our personal reality with him through free will and conscious choice about which thoughts we cherish in our minds.

Through the synchronicity of the mind-consciousness, we know that any modification or level of consciousness that a person places in unity with a mental field that shares similar energy will project that energy state into their perception of reality.

This is why, when we wake up in a bad mood, it seems like everything that happens throughout the day is negative: we encounter all sorts of unpleasant situations. We're late to work, argue with a colleague, spill coffee on our shirt, lose our wallet... everything feels off. Your mental state is connected to a corresponding body that includes "external" events of the same class, reinforcing the identification with the contents of your mind.

That's why Henry Ford's saying, "Whether you think you can,

or think you can't, you're right," is so profound. Now, you might ask: what is the most effective method to control the mind? Controlling the mind requires elevating our consciousness. This means we become aware of both our brain hemispheres, or, as we commonly call it, our conscious and subconscious mind.

Scientifically, there are three ways to alter consciousness, meaning to access and synchronize the two hemispheres of the brain. According to the theories of legendary scientists and inventors like Itshak Bentov, we know that the subconscious is actually the right hemisphere of the brain, which functions as a holistic element, free from criticism, non-verbal, and non-structured. It accepts everything the left hemisphere processes—this is the part that filters, categorizes, and assigns meaning to all the information coming from external stimuli. It's the self-cognitive, verbal, and critical part, using linear reasoning.

The left hemisphere is responsible for filtering, categorizing, and assigning meaning to everything before it reaches the right hemisphere. Once we access the right hemisphere, it "accepts everything" as absolute truth and executes it as such.

Therefore, in order to achieve what we aim for, we must send the right information to our right hemisphere. What is the right information? Your vision of the "self" fully realized.

This vision only occurs when there is synchronization between the two hemispheres of the brain. There are three known methods to achieve this synchronization. Once this union occurs, it's said that a person reaches higher states of consciousness that even transcend space-time dimensions. Let's explore these methods:

1. Hypnosis

This technique allows direct access to the sensory motors of the cortex and to the pleasure stimulation centers, located in the lower part of the right hemisphere (the emotional part). If we can distract the left hemisphere—meaning if we manage to stop stimulating it and leave it "at rest" through boredom or a semi-dormant state (such as when we transition from wakefulness to sleep)—we can induce external suggestions or stimuli that the brain will "allow" to pass into the subconscious without the left hemisphere interfering. In other words, these suggestions can go straight into the subconscious (right hemisphere) without being filtered by the left hemisphere.

This is why hypnotic therapies—performed by professionals—can have impressive healing effects, as the right hemisphere is "hypnotized," and the subconscious takes control of the mind. These hypnotic states can be personally accessed through meditation.

2. Meditation

All meditation techniques require concentration. This means the ability to maintain attention for long periods. Meditation is a voluntary action to learn the art of controlling the mind, which means being able to recognize each and every thought that arises in the mind and seeing them completely detached.

There are many types of meditation techniques that can be practiced today. For practical reasons, I will only mention how to prepare to acquire the habit of meditation. For more detailed explanations of all the meditation techniques available, I recommend Jacobo Grinberg-Zylberbaum's book *Meditations*, where he presents over 20 types of meditation, from pranayama, autolytic meditation, vipassana, siddha, transcendental, Kabbalistic, Olmec, etc.

To enter the fascinating world of meditation, it is necessary to practice it once or twice a day, for a minimum of 20 minutes per session. Grinberg mentions that the best time to meditate is early in the morning or at dusk. However, we should not abandon the practice if we can't do it at those times. Any time of day is better than no practice at all.

It's important to meditate in a quiet place, free from distractions like external noises, insects, or other disturbances. The room should have minimal items and be clean. It's recommended to wear comfortable and loose clothing.

The ideal posture for meditation is to sit on the floor on a comfortable surface, such as a cushion or soft rug, with legs crossed and the back straight. You can also use a chair or armchair, as long as your feet are grounded. It is generally not recommended to meditate lying down, as there is a risk of falling asleep. If sitting is not possible, try to stay awake and consciously active.

Another key aspect is not to meditate on an empty stomach, nor when it's too full. The ideal is to feel comfortable and neither hungry nor overstuffed. Once you're seated in position and ready to meditate, the next step is to fully focus on either a physical object or a biological process like breathing.

3. Directed Attention or Biofeedback

This method is interesting because it applies the cognitive powers of the left hemisphere intentionally to access the right hemisphere. Instead of suppressing the activity of the left brain through hypnosis or "turning it off" through meditation to access the right hemisphere, the technique of directed attention teaches the right hemisphere to visualize the desired outcome and then recognize the feelings associated with visualizing the successful state of that desired outcome.

Scientifically, this means that through visualization, a process used by the left hemisphere (the rational side), we instruct the right hemisphere (the unifying side) to associate a feeling (trying to connect with the lower cortex of the brain, which is connected to neurons related to pleasure) to transmit the sense of fulfillment, making this process tend to "materialize" the result.

Biofeedback is a technique widely used, especially for treating chronic diseases. By focusing your consciousness on the part of the body where you feel pain and applying mindfulness techniques, the patient can send feelings of peace and comfort to the "damaged" area for a constant and determined period, until symptoms—and even pain—disappear.

You've likely heard of the famous Law of Attraction, which became widely known among personal development advocates: "Visualize your dreams as clearly as possible, then identify with that feeling as if it's already yours, and what you desire will manifest in your reality." I assume that the theory behind the Law of Attraction is based on this method.

The problem is that personal development advocates forgot to mention to their fervent followers that the small detail is that it's not about an easy manifestation, nor a means of obtaining simple material goods. Biofeedback is a biological and metaphysical process that requires serious and intense training to yield true results. It's an effort of focused attention that can take years of training. The mind control mechanisms are serious techniques, and misuse of them can lead to severe consequences, so I recommend using them with great judgment and maturity.

Part Three | Establish Systems

We've finally reached the practical part of developing discipline.

I've left this section for last because I believe that, in order to truly anchor discipline as a lifestyle, you first need to understand the main obstacles that are holding you back.

Once you've identified the enemy, you can reprogram your mind to assist you in developing that long-desired discipline and seeing it as a way of life, rather than an "external" tool.

With the right mindset and optimal energy levels, materializing your dreams through disciplined actions will become a piece of cake.

Chapter 19 | Powerful Routines

Although I'm not a fan of rigid schedules for daily life, I do believe it's important to develop consistent daily routines that align with your goals and the lifestyle you want to achieve.

For example, your daily routine should include time for exercise, time to work on your goals, time to rest, and time to interact with your family. Finding a balance in how you structure and plan your time is key to ensuring you don't neglect any aspect of your life.

It's also important to consider the lifestyle you aspire to. When I talk about "lifestyle," I mean making a conscious decision to do things that make you happy and help you fulfill your goals.

Many people confuse "lifestyle" with the activity of consuming. For instance, social media and TV commercials always "sell" different lifestyles: the glamorous one, the minimalist one, the sporty one, the vegan one, the traveler one... and so on. It seems like the defining factor of a lifestyle is what you consume, and that's what you become.

There's some truth to that, but in my opinion, lifestyle has a much deeper meaning. Lifestyle shouldn't focus on consumption, but rather on attitude, ideas, discoveries... and most importantly, on a **search for something more.**

A good lifestyle is the search for the *Self*. It's about continuously seeking those experiences that bring you true joy in life; it's a search that keeps your desire alive to become a person of deep values, one who seeks to transcend a meaningless routine based solely on consumption and survival.

If we start by establishing our daily routine based on this search to be and transcend, the activities you choose to do throughout the day will become more intentional and will hold more meaning for you.

Suddenly, waking up at six in the morning to meditate or work out before heading to work no longer feels like a chore or a trendy activity that everyone is doing, so you have to add it to your to-do list.

Let's take a look at the routines of some famous people and how they choose their activities based on their lifestyles: In an interview with *Business Insider*, the second richest man in the world, Jeff Bezos, shared his daily routine after stepping down as CEO of Amazon to focus on his company, Blue Origin.

Bezos starts his day without needing an alarm clock. He likes to sleep 8 hours a night. When he wakes up, he prefers to begin his mornings calmly and without rush, taking time to enjoy a cup of coffee and read the newspaper.

Then, he dedicates time to journaling and working out in the gym. When it comes to work, he prefers to schedule his most important meetings before noon. "If I have to make a complex decision or the meeting is going to be particularly difficult, I like to schedule it at 10 a.m.," he told *Business Insider*.

Bezos doesn't like to schedule tough meetings in the afternoon when his energy is lower. If a meeting comes up after 5 p.m., he prefers to move it to the next morning to ensure he's in the best mental state. He also emphasizes the importance of rest:

"For me, sleep is a priority. If I sleep well, I think better, I have more energy, and my mood is better," he stated in the same interview.

He also says that as a high-level executive, his job involves making only a small number of very important decisions. Making thousands of small decisions all the time doesn't make sense to him and is a waste of energy. As you can see, this example clearly highlights Bezos' priorities in life.

Let's consider another example: Cristiano Ronaldo, one of the best football players of all time. Cristiano's routine, as expected, is highly specific to his lifestyle, which is 100% focused on sports. He trains for about 4 hours a day, takes 5 90-minute naps, and eats 6 times a day to maintain optimal physical performance.

Of course, we've seen examples of rich people who have the power to decide how to spend their time. You might be wondering: what about people who can't afford such luxuries? After all, not everyone has the privilege of Jeff Bezos waking up in the morning without worries or the need for an alarm clock. The reality for most people is quite different.

Most of us have to wake up at 6 a.m. to go to work, or even earlier if our workplace is far from home. You have kids to take care of and take to school, or a dog to walk before heading to work.

You also can't spend five hours in the gym like Cristiano Ronaldo, who has the fame and money to organize his time however he pleases.

So, what about us, the ordinary people? Are we free to choose? Although it may seem surreal, we too can choose and design our routines:

- **We can choose** to wake up without an alarm clock.
- **We can decide** to stop working for a boss and become our own boss.

- **We can set** daily routines that allow us to reach our goals and carry them out consistently.

As I mentioned earlier, it doesn't require an extremely rigid schedule. The key is to always dedicate time during the day—whenever works for you—to the activities that are important for achieving your goals.

Chapter 20 | The Power of Microtasks

I must admit, I'm a huge fan of microtasks because their power lies in being something you can do immediately, with minimal effort, but that little by little leads you to the result you're aiming for.

Many people who aspire to achieve something freeze when they think about all the things they need to do to get there. It paralyzes them, and then it's no surprise that they end up not starting at all.

But what would happen if instead of focusing on all the activities I need to do to achieve something, I focused on just one thing each day, and the next day on another? Let's say my goal is to write a book. Instead of taking on the difficult task of writing a set number of words, for example, "I will write 3,000 words a day," which is about six pages, I would commit to writing just one page a day.

The brain will feel less overwhelmed by the task, and it will be easier to find time during the day to write one page rather than six. In fact, if one page isn't possible, you can reduce the goal even further and commit to writing one paragraph a day. In the end, doing "ant tasks" in a set amount of time will lead you to complete your goal faster than if you assign yourself large tasks that are nearly impossible to sustain.

I've implemented this method, and it really works well. At the beginning, when I set ambitious goals, for example, exercising one hour a day every morning, I noticed that I only managed to stick to the first few exercise sessions. But as soon as an inconvenience came up, I would quit and tell myself, "I'll start again tomorrow," which rarely happened.

On the other hand, if I reduce my goal to 20 minutes of exercise a day (instead of one hour), my brain doesn't feel as overwhelmed by the task of "making space" in my daily routine for that amount of time. Plus, it offers more flexibility to choose the time of day when I can fit it in.

In the end, the impact of exercising 20 minutes every day for a month is 600 minutes of exercise per month, which is a much greater benefit than exercising one hour a week, which would only result in 240 minutes at the end of the month. With 20 minutes a day, you ensure a solid routine that is easy to achieve and, over time, will deliver better results than waiting for that one hour each week, which is harder to maintain and much more likely to be abandoned.

Are you starting to see the power of MICRO?

This is what James Clear talks about in his book *Atomic Habits*, describing the "Law of Compound Effect": making small incremental changes over time that generate a much larger benefit than big transformations.

I like to compare this concept to the work of ants, who build their empires piece by piece, but never stop. You see them walking tirelessly, carrying tiny bits of leaves, one after the other in an unstoppable dance, until suddenly, without you realizing it, they've built their massive nest.

So, if you're struggling to start a task, break it down into smaller pieces... and start with the *micro*!

Chapter 21 | Create a Winning System

Let's return to our conversation about what you want to achieve in life. Do you want to succeed in what you set out to do consistently? Achieve financial freedom, the ideal state of health, and have enough time for your loved ones and hobbies? Then stop focusing only on goals. Yes, you read that right. Maybe right now you think it's a joke, but this is a serious proposal.

So, have all these productivity and personal development gurus been wrong? They've taught us time and again that setting goals is one of the keys to success. I, too, confess to having believed this and even promoted it in my previous books.

I kept believing it not long ago until one day I came across a quote from the famous American author and comedian Scott Adams:

"Goals are for losers, systems are for winners."

I had to stop, reflect, and read it again to understand the meaning of this quote. My first reaction was to dismiss it: How could this be? If literally, the entire personal development world is built around the importance of setting and achieving goals... Isn't that the ultimate purpose of the personal development industry?

But the more thoughtful side of me finally saw sense in what I was observing over and over again after years of working in multinational companies. People always set goals. Sometimes we achieve some of our goals very well, and other times we fail. Why? Because we don't act consistently and constantly to maintain the same results.

Let's return to the famous example of weight loss. Perhaps someone sets a goal to lose 50 pounds, and let's say they achieve it. Everything is wonderful up until this point, but if that person simply put in the effort once, what are their chances of maintaining that weight consistently over time?

If we're honest, we know there's a very high probability that this person will gain weight back at some point and even return to their previous weight if they haven't changed anything in their habits to maintain it. But what happens if that person establishes a healthy lifestyle and consistently sustains those habits? Most likely, they will maintain their weight in the long term.

So how do we maintain consistency without failing? *Voilà!* We need a **system**. A method, a way of doing things that we know will work for us every time, or at least almost always.

Interestingly, it's the same thing I observed in business. When there were no clear and defined processes, people wouldn't take responsibility for their actions. Without a series of steps to follow, most acted based on their own personal opinions about how the work should be done.

As a result, there was no way to measure the success of a process or system, leading to erratic results: sometimes it worked, sometimes it didn't. It depended on who performed which steps, and when that person left the company, a gap formed in the process. What was consistent, however, was the increase in costs and the low profitability. Another person would come with different ideas and ways of doing things, and as expected, the process changed again. There was no way to measure results, which created high costs for the company with no benefit.

Therefore, more than the goal itself, it is much more important to develop systems and processes to help you achieve it. Interesting, right? And the reason is simple. When we only set goals but have no system to back them up, you may start with a lot of energy and motivation, but over time that energy gets depleted, and since you're not doing things consistently (the same way every day), at some point, you stop… and the problems begin.

Notice how chains like McDonald's or companies like Apple are so successful. No matter where in the world you go, you'll always receive the same product, of the same quality, with the same format.

Imagine, according to the latest statistics (Statista, 2023), McDonald's employs 150,000 people worldwide. How do they achieve such a level of consistency in service, product, infrastructure, marketing, etc.?

If each person has an average of 20,000 to 60,000 thoughts per day, imagine the chaos it would be if each one acted based on their own thoughts about how to perform a task at McDonald's. It would be madness! Probably, the chain would not have achieved the global success and coverage it has today, and maintained over the years. This is why it's so important to establish systems that help us consistently achieve our goals.

Okay, now it's understood, but you might ask, what the heck is a system? I really like a popular definition used in business very often:

SYSTEM = Save YourSelf Time Energy & Money.

I don't know who came up with this phrase, but it's brilliant and describes very well what systems do for us. I know the term *system* might sound technical. In the end, a system is nothing more than a set of processes, people, technologies, and interfaces interacting harmoniously to produce a result.

Let's use an easy example. Let's say you want to open a pizzeria, and your goal is to produce 20 pizzas in an hour. How do you achieve this? Let's say, at first, you make one pizza at a time yourself.

I bet that by the third pizza, you'd give up. Probably, none of them would look the same. Maybe for the first one, you used 40 grams of mozzarella, three tomatoes, two salamis, and six spinach leaves (ugh, let's change spinach to basil... I can't imagine a pizza with spinach). Anyway, an hour passes and you're way behind your goal.

Then, you analyze what you could do better. You decide to have your best friend help you prepare the pizzas. Now there are four hands instead of two. Great, but it turns out that even though the pizza preparation is faster, you only have one oven that can hold two pizzas at a time; considering each pizza needs 25 minutes to cook, you realize you can only make four pizzas per hour.

Okay, we need to keep analyzing our system. Eventually, you decide it would be good to invest in two more ovens. Then, you realize you need one more person to take orders, another to serve the pizzas, someone to clean... in the end, doing it all yourself or with just two people isn't enough.

You need to hire a waiter, someone to handle purchasing ingredients, someone to handle administration, and define all the important processes: How do you order the raw materials? How often? What are the opening hours? How do you start workdays? What's the sequence for pizza preparation?

In the end, starting your own pizzeria is not just about having the dream and the goal; it's about building the system and the processes that will make the goal achievable consistently.

How to Create Mini Systems in Daily Life

In businesses, we clearly visualize this, but when it comes to our personal lives, we see things through different lenses. We think processes and systems are boring concepts from businesses and that we don't need any of that in our daily lives, right?

Dear reader, I regret to inform you of bad news: the reality is that processes and systems are not only still relevant, they're *crucial,* especially if you want to achieve your dreams.

Here are several examples of small processes and systems I've implemented to achieve some of my goals:

1. Taking time to identify my daily tasks

Every night, before going to bed, I make a list of the tasks I need to do the next day. I also include essential activities like eating, sleeping, exercising, spending time with the kids, etc.

2. Prioritizing tasks

I always try to focus on completing three important tasks each day, whether it's dedicating time to writing, a family event, an important appointment, or any other relevant or urgent activity that day.

3. Creating a fixed schedule

This has worked really well for me, especially in creating consistent routines. I assign a time for each important task. For example, I always schedule my exercise time in the morning after dropping the kids off at school. This is when I'm at my best and when I've seen the best results.

. . .

4. Establishing morning and evening routines

Think about what activities you can combine to create a consistent routine. For example, I found it very useful to establish my morning routine as follows: wake up at the same time (6:00 am), thank God for a new day, wash my face, prepare warm water with lemon and a little baking soda, get dressed in my workout clothes (which I prepared the night before), wake the kids, make breakfast, get them ready for school, and once they leave, I immediately start exercising or go for a jog. I follow the exact same steps like this every day from 6:00 to 8:30 am.

After 8:30, I'm ready to begin the rest of the day. In the evening, I like to incorporate relaxing routines like reading a book, writing, preparing things for the next day, and meditating.

5. Automatize what I can

I love automating everything I can. For example, I often automate my social media posts. With a program called Canva,* I can schedule the posts I want to publish on certain days, design several posts in bulk, write the text, schedule the dates, and forget about spending time posting on Instagram for five days.

I use my Google Calendar to schedule all my appointments and always ask it to send me reminders a day before to prepare for important meetings. Of course, I use all kinds of appliances that help automate daily chores at home (washing machine, dryer, dishwasher, robot vacuum...). For these tasks, I'm a fan of robots!

I schedule my emails to send automatic replies to each client or person who writes to me asking for information or making initial contact. When it comes to automation, I try to choose the tasks that I find less pleasant or those that are important but that I don't want to spend most of my time on.

---

* Visit www.canva.com.

. . .

6. I review and document my processes

It sounds boring, but essentially, I like to occasionally review how I structure my schedules and activities to evaluate whether I am truly heading in the direction I want to achieve, or if something needs to be changed. For example, as a writer, I've set the goal of publishing at least two books per year. Obviously, my daily routine must contain time blocks dedicated to writing.

We know that plans can change and that we need to remain flexible, but the beauty of having a well-established process (or routine) is that it doesn't matter if sometimes you don't follow them to the letter; as long as you stay consistent, it will always be easier to implement them again.

7. Delegate

Delegating work is important. I know it's not easy, especially if you're a mom and want to take care of everything yourself (for example, organizing your children's life, keeping a spotless house, working, having a social life, exercising, staying up to date with every family event, taking care of the garden...) it can be quite overwhelming.

It's not about being *Superwoman* or *Superman,* but being honest with ourselves and evaluating what activities make sense for us and where we should invest our time.

As a general rule, I delegate everything I feel isn't important for me to do myself (for example, fixing the garden, washing clothes, cleaning windows) or even things I know someone else can do better than me. For my books, I hire a professional cover designer, for financial matters, I hire an accountant or consultant. I try to be selective about the things I decide to do myself.

Hold on a moment... you've probably noticed that I'm now

contradicting myself because in the earlier chapters, I criticize the educational system precisely for its rigidity and inflexibility, and how it destroys free will when it comes to our own development and learning.

Well, despite being a fan of systems, I still think the same: there is a huge difference between following systems imposed by others and defining and executing **your own systems**, the ones that work for *you*.

In fact, one of the reasons why the current educational system has been so successfully implemented from generation to generation is because its gears form an almost perfect system. So perfect that society doesn't notice that traditional school is the first prison you're subjected to from a very young age.

I don't know if you've seen a very famous image circulating on social media, where on the left, you see children entering a machine; the children look happy, and their environment is full of colors and fantasy. Once they enter the machine (which resembles one of those industrial machines that processes products in bulk), all the children come out with a somber look, all dressed in the same uniform, holding their "titles" or qualifications. It may look like a fictional drawing, but it is closer to reality than we're willing to admit.

Now you know: systems are not simply boring and technical things that companies use to implement their activities, but they can also be a powerful tool and your best allies when it comes to establishing self-discipline that truly helps you achieve all your goals.

Chapter 22 | Throw Away the Concept of "Multitasking"

The concept of "multitasking" is not a good idea when you're looking to develop the habit of discipline permanently. The problem with multitasking is that you're unable to focus on any activity in particular while you're trying to execute multiple tasks at the same time.

It's a terrible practice, totally overrated even in the workforce, where they often promote this supposed skill as something desirable for candidates applying for certain jobs.

The final consequence of multitasking is always negative. No one can write an email consciously while attending an online conference and simultaneously listening to a YouTube video... As the saying goes, "No one serves two masters," let alone three or more.

You might think—consciously and in good faith—that you're paying attention to everything, but in reality, one thing will always be dominant. The problem is that even though one thing dominates, the distractions from the others mean that you won't do any of the tasks really well because you're *dividing your attention.*

I've been a direct witness to how this practice fails on all levels.

I have two young children. I've played the role of the "multitasking mom" that's so promoted on social media: the one who changes diapers while cooking, while talking on the phone... I assure you that at some point the rice burns, I stop paying attention to the call to finish changing the diaper, or I leave both things half done when my child cries or asks me to get a toy from the cupboard.

Biologist and anthropologist Gregory Bateson, in his book *Steps to an Ecology of Mind*, proposes that as individual organisms interacting in a much larger ecosystem, we are only capable of conceptualizing the representation of "the whole" in small parts; there is, to some extent, a compartmentalization of the mind that is seemingly necessary for us to operate optimally in everyday life.

Bateson claims that there is a "semi-impermeable" connection between active consciousness and the totality of what we call the "mind." Only a very small part of the total information interacting in what we call the extended mind seems to be attributed to what we know as the screen of consciousness.

To make it easier to understand, imagine your brain is like a television, and what we call "the mind" is the software that contains all the information of the channels. Your brain can only capture a particular set of frequency waves containing information from a specific channel. That's why when you watch television, you can only see one channel at a time, even though thousands of channels are being broadcast to millions of people all over the world at that same instant. However, you can only see the channel you've chosen at that moment.

I make this analogy to emphasize that, from our biological construction, we are designed to focus on a limited reality—what our consciousness chooses to focus on. To summarize, let's review once more the disadvantages of "multitasking":

- **Lower efficiency and performance:**

Even though the idea behind multitasking is to achieve greater efficiency by "saving time," in reality, we are causing the opposite effect. Constantly switching our attention between different tasks leads to us losing time as we refocus on the task that was left pending. This ultimately slows down the process of completing tasks.

- **Increased stress:** The more things you try to manage at the same time, the higher the percentage of anxiety and stress you generate unnecessarily. At this point, we know that stress has a devastating effect on our health, as it negatively alters all the biological processes of the body's regeneration.

- **Difficulty learning:** Do you remember that I mentioned that traditional education can be one of the most dangerous enemies of true discipline? It's precisely because when we want to learn something new correctly, we need to focus our attention for a long period of time. Therefore, cutting the time dedicated to learning something into small fragments (for example, in school, one hour per class; at work, one hour per subject, etc.) can make learning slower and less effective.

- **No space for creativity:** This ties into the previous point. When you don't have time to properly learn a craft or skill, you'll also find it harder to generate new ideas. Your brain is too busy and overwhelmed with information, trying to manage the simultaneous load of different stimuli, and in the end, it has no time to think "outside the box," which limits your creative space.

. . .

- **Reduced attention span:** In the age of social media and instant communication, we can clearly see how the use of these technologies for long-term information consumption is causing serious cognitive problems for tasks that require focus and a prolonged period of time to complete. In fact, the concept of social media is taking multitasking to the extreme for the mind. Platforms like TikTok expose the brain to millions of instant pieces of information in seconds. In just a few minutes, you can watch hundreds of videos on all kinds of content, which generates that feeling of addiction in the brain; the anxiety of consuming more. The same happens when we try to do several things at once. In reality, we don't give full attention to anything we're doing, which can have negative consequences for our optimal performance in day-to-day tasks.

Chapter 23 | Visualize the Practice Before Executing

During my professional career, there were many occasions when I had to prepare presentations for executives, conduct training sessions, or speak in public. At first, all of this felt quite intimidating, especially when starting from scratch.

How do you turn a blank sheet of paper into a business presentation, a training session, or a speech? My favorite technique was to first **imagine it**. I would visualize the presentation, the key messages I wanted to convey, the graphics I planned to show, the colors of the visuals, and the emotions I aimed to evoke with my message.

I imagined myself giving the presentation, emphasizing the key points repeatedly. I envisioned colleagues' reactions, tough questions, criticisms, and even their impressions. I mentally prepared all my responses.

I aimed to visualize the presentation at least three times as vividly as possible. I would do this at any moment of the day: while washing dishes, showering, or jogging. I played out the presentation in my mind over and over again.

Once it felt "familiar," I would transfer it to paper or prepare the presentation in PowerPoint. Essentially, I brought the presentation from the realm of abstract thought into the material world.

This technique has worked exceptionally well for me, even now when writing my books. I first imagine the outline, the structure of the book, and the concepts I want to explain. I picture the cover, the colors, and the feelings I want to convey. Then I simply sit down and materialize in the physical world what I had envisioned.

When planning my beach wedding, I used the same technique. I explored many ideas and locations, looked at numerous photos, and then began shaping my ideal wedding. I vividly imagined every detail repeatedly: the color of the sea, how the dress would look, the type of flowers I wanted, the arrangements, the lights, the food I would serve, and the experience I wanted my guests to have. I imagined it over and over again until, when the opportunity came to hire a wedding planner, I could precisely describe my ideas and literally materialized my dream wedding.

I could provide more examples, but I believe you get the idea. In his book *The Little Book of Talent*, Daniel Coyle discusses this technique and how music schools and elite athletes use it to enhance their students' skills. He refers to it as the "engraving method." It involves visualizing the practice you want to master repeatedly, down to the smallest detail, and then replicating it.

To be successful with this practice, you need an intense connection: observing and listening so attentively that you feel as though you are performing the skill in reality. Once you feel that connection... execute and repeat.

It's incredible how the repetition of simple activities over a determined period can transform the ordinary into the *extraordinary*. We see countless examples of this powerful yet simple law.

Look at how great athletes, musicians, chefs, and virtually any outstanding professional in their field practice their craft over and over again, perfecting it a little more each time. The greatest skills are those executed with extraordinary precision; this level of rigor and excellence can only be achieved through consistent practice.

Stephen King, the acclaimed American horror novelist, revealed in his autobiographical book *On Writing: A Memoir of the Craft* that his goal was to write 2,000 words a day, resulting in 180,000 words in three months—perfect for a book in his genre.

The famous tennis player Venus Williams has also stated in numerous interviews that she owes her success to discipline: "Motivation is temporary. Discipline creates habits and routines, and routines become who you are daily."

Writer and cartoonist Scott Adams mentions in his book *How to Fail at Almost Everything and Still Win Big* that people often underestimate the power of positively visualizing a goal they want to achieve and dedicating the necessary hours to attain it. Most people tend to give up before reaching the level of expertise needed to excel in a particular activity.

> *"Free yourself from the chains of an oppressive reality. What is real to you is what you imagine and feel. If you wisely imagine your dreams, you might just achieve them."*
>
> —SCOTT ADAMS

Chapter 24 | Fall in Love with the Process

Let's be honest—when we start any activity or project, what we crave the most is seeing results... as quickly as possible! You begin a diet to lose weight and expect to see results in just a few days. When they don't appear, your motivation drops significantly, leaving you questioning whether to continue. You might even give up entirely, thinking there's no point in "suffering" without visible benefits.

In the era of hyperconnectivity and instant gratification, it has become even harder to develop the patience required to focus on tasks for extended periods, even when you know those tasks will lead to the desired outcome.

The problem lies in how nearly every activity that used to take time—like writing a letter, shopping for fresh produce, cooking, exercising, or reading—has been replaced by instant solutions. With social media and *online* services, everything is just a click away.

Feeling too tired to cook after work? UberEats is the answer. Want to reconnect with a long-lost friend? Send a WhatsApp filled with emojis. Need to do your weekly grocery shopping? A few clicks on any online store will not only complete your list but also deliver it to your doorstep.

But what's the downside of this instant gratification for simple things? The issue isn't the technology itself but rather the effect that immediacy has on our brains and our ability to learn and build habits that foster good discipline.

Dr. Caroline Leaf, a neuroscientist and expert in brain neuroplasticity, addresses this in her book *Switch On Your Brain.* She explains how multitasking and erratic, unfocused thoughts negatively affect the brain's proper functioning.

When we dedicate ourselves to completing a specific task without rushing and with full concentration, it calms the mind. This calmness enhances the brain's ability to form the neural connections needed to learn and reinforce that skill. Dr. Leaf notes:

"The ability to calm your mind, focus your attention on the current task, capture your thoughts, and discard distractions is an excellent skill that God has placed within you."

The key, then, lies in the focused attention you give to every activity—even every thought. For example, high-performance athletes enjoy their training routines. Renowned U.S. gymnast Simone Biles has mentioned in several interviews that she loves training because it allows her to focus on perfecting her skills.

It's the process that allows us to develop the necessary skills to master any activity.

The Role of Time

> *"There's a distinction between what society thinks is valuable and what a person in their heart feels is valuable."*
>
> —PAOLA KNECHT

Time, as we perceive it, is an illusion—a human invention to impose order and logic on events that seem to unfold linearly. For instance, we think of aging as following a linear pattern.

Each of us has 24 hours in a day. No one receives more or fewer hours. We all share this universal perception of time. What we consider our "present" is merely a conscious state in the moment. Therefore, the only true reality is the present moment; everything else is either a memory of what we call the past or projections of thoughts into a continuous "future."

Pause for a moment and reflect on how you perceive time. You'll notice something peculiar: the perception of time passing changes based on your mood and personal circumstances. A child and an adult perceive the passage of time differently. For a child, time drags on, leading to impatience. For an adult, time often feels like it's moving too quickly.

When we're bored, time feels empty, and we think we need to fill that emptiness with something. On the other hand, when we're engaged in something we love, time seems to vanish in the blink of an eye. In a meditative state, time appears to lose its power, and we simply enjoy being *present*.

This demonstrates that time is indeed a human creation—a simple tool to measure our journey through life for the sake of collective organization. As such, we have the power to alter our experience of this fictional construct.

It's worth investing this tool called time in pursuits that truly matter, leading to a fulfilling and meaningful life. You don't need to pay for expensive productivity courses or sign up for a time-management *MasterClass*.

These are merely products designed for a market that capitalizes on people's anxiety and willingness to spend money to reclaim something that inherently belongs to them—a natural part of human design: your own perception of time and the power to decide how to use it.

Potentially, you have absolute control over how you manage your time. It all comes down to consciously deciding how to invest it. The choices you make daily, even minute by minute, shape the *reality* your brain perceives.

You can choose to engage in activities that make you happy and bring you closer to the lifestyle you desire, or you can let this priceless opportunity slip away, surrendering to daily distractions. As always, the choice is *yours*.

Chapter 25 | The Magic of the Subconscious

To close, I want to remind you of the key ingredient for achieving the life you deeply desire and are willing to discipline yourself for. That ingredient is the ally within us all, the one responsible for keeping us alive and managing countless processes and operations in our daily lives without us even realizing it: our subconscious.

Please revisit Chapter 18, where I describe proven and effective methods for intentionally connecting with your subconscious. It's worth recalling the words of Neville Goddard, author of *Feeling is the Secret*:

"Through the power of thought, imagination, feeling, and the freedom we have to choose how to occupy our minds, humankind has control over Creation."

Imagine your mind as a light bulb radiating light to illuminate an entire room. This light represents your usual attention—it shines, but only superficially and without focus. It's warm, but its purpose is limited to diffuse illumination.

Now, imagine applying a highly concentrated energy source (attention, focus, and discipline) to that light bulb, transforming it into a laser beam. Laser light is immensely powerful because it concentrates significant amounts of energy in a small, focused area. Lasers are used in various industries—for cutting through thick metals and diamonds, performing surgeries, and even measuring vast distances.

Standard light, like the one we use to illuminate rooms, is incoherent and polychromatic. It spreads in all directions and consists of multiple colors. Its wavelengths are scattered and inconsistent, making its illumination broad but imprecise.

If you examined this light under a microscope, you'd see its waves vary in length, size, and color, traveling chaotically in all directions. This is why it's called *incoherent* light.

In contrast, laser light consists of waves of the same length, color, and amplitude, moving in a single direction within a confined space. This is known as *coherent* light.

It's fascinating to compare the behavior of light with that of our minds. Our "everyday" minds are similarly incoherent, erratic, and unfocused, which makes it challenging to achieve our goals consistently.

APPLYING SELF-DISCIPLINE TO OUR LIVES IS LIKE APPLYING LASER LIGHT TO OUR MINDS.

Focused attention helps us stay present in what we're doing. When combined with systems designed to maintain that laser focus, we unlock a profound secret—the key that opens the gate to the mind's potential: focused, systematic attention governed by the supreme force of love.

I HOPE THIS BOOK HAS FULFILLED ITS PRIMARY PURPOSE: TO remind you of what you already know—that you *are* everything you wish to become. The only thing separating who you are from who you want to be is as simple as the power of decision and focused attention.

We are constantly fighting against dark forces that aim to keep us from discovering that we are beings of light, powerful entities with cosmic consciousness. Once we connect with this truth, nothing will stand in the way of our future endeavors.

I'd Love Your Feedback

I would be truly grateful if you could share your thoughts on *The Secrets of Discipline*. Your review is an invaluable gift that will help me refine my message and ensure I offer you the best in future publications.

You can write a review on the platform where you purchased the book or send me a personal note at:

info@paolaknecht.com

Also, feel free to connect with me on social media!

- **Instagram**: @paolaknecht_author
- **X** (formerly Twitter): @PaolaKnecht
- **LinkedIn**: Paola Knecht

Thank you for being part of this journey!

About the Author

Paola Knecht is an author, mindset and transformation coach, and therapist in clinical training, committed to personal development and holistic well-being. With five books published in Spanish and English — including The Success Mindset and Awaken Your Inner Genie — her writing has accompanied readers around the world on the path toward a more conscious and fulfilling life.

With over fifteen years of experience in engineering and strategic management at globally recognized companies, Paola chose to redirect her expertise toward what truly moves her: understanding the human mind and accompanying people in their transformation. Today she combines her coaching practice with advanced studies in clinical psychology and psychotherapy, deepening her understanding of the scientific and therapeutic side of change.

She lives in Switzerland with her husband and children, and works with an international audience.

To follow her publications and learn more about her work, visit: paolaknecht.com

Coaching and accompaniment at savia.paolaknecht.com

Monthly reflections at paolaknecht.com/newsletter

Bibliography

Adams, Scott. How to Fail at Almost Everything and Still Win Big. United Kingdom :Penguin Random House Business, 2016.

Ali, Marium (2023): «How many years does a typical user spend on social media?»,https://www.aljazeera.com/news/2023/6/30/how-many-years-does-a-typical-user-spend-on-social-media#, accessed 15 June 2024.

American Psychological Association (2024): «Resilience», https://www.apa.org/topics/resilience, accessed 16 May 2023.

Bateson, Gregory. Steps to an ecology of the mind. Chicago: The University of Chicago Press, 2000.

Bentov, Itzhak. A Brief Tour of Higher Consciousness: A Cosmic Book on the Mechanics of Creation. Vermont: Destiny Books, 2000.

Bryant Conant, James. The Child, the Parent, and the State. Cambridge, Mass. Harvard University Press, 1959.

Calin, Ainé (2024): «A day in the life of Je1 Bezos, the second richest person in the world», https://www.businessinsider.com/je1-bezos-daily-routine-2017-7, accessed 10 June 2024.

Coyle, Daniel. El pequeño libro del talento. Editorial Conecta [versión Kindle].

Delgado, Lucas (2023): «La rutina de CR7: 3 horas de entrenamiento, 5 siestas y hasta 6 comidas diarias», https://www.sportlife.es/noticias/rutina-cr7-3-horas-entrenamiento-5-siestas-hasta-6-comidas-diarias-bzm_281096_102.html, accessed 9 June 2024.

Dimasio, Antonio. Descartes' Error: Emotion, Reason. London: Penguin Books, 2005.

D'Ors, Pablo. Biografía del silencio. Galaxia Gutenberg [versión Kindle].

Elhai, J. D.; Levine, J. C.; Dvorak, R. D.; & Hall, B. J. (2016). «Fear of Missing Out, Need for Touch, Anxiety and Depression Are Related to Problematic Smartphone Use». Computers in Human Behavior, 63, pp. 509-516.

European Environment Agency (2024): «Emerging chemical risk I Europe. "PFAS"», https://www.eea.europa.eu/publications/emerging-chemical-risks-in-europe/emerging-chemical-risks-in-europe, accessed 9 September 2024.

Fardouly, J.; Diedrichs, P. C.; Vartanian, L. R.; & Halliwell, E. (2015).«Social Comparisons on Social Media: The Impact of Facebook on Young Women's Body Image Concerns and Mood». Body Image, 13, pp. 38-45.

Gatto, John Taylor. Dumbing Us Down - 25th Anniversary Edition. New Society Publishers [versión Kindle].

Goggins, David. Can't Hurt Me: Master Your Mind and Defy the Odds. Lioncrest Publishing [versión Kindle].

Goddard, Neville. Feeling is the Secret. Mumbai (India): Sanage Publishing House, 2020.

Gómez, Mar (2023): «Este es el pueblo más frío del mundo», https://www.eltiempo.es/noticias/el-lugar-mas-frio-del-mundo, accessed 12 May 2024.

Neufeld, Gordon PH.D. and Maté, Gabor M.D. Hold on To Your Kids: Why Parents Need to Matter More Than Peers: Ballantine Books Trade Paperback Edition, New York, 2014.

Greene, Robert. The Laws of Human Nature. London: Penguin Random House, 2018.

Grinberg-Zylberbaum, Jacobo. El Yo como idea. México: Instituto Nacional para el Estudio de la Conciencia, 1994.

____________________. La teoría sintérgica, México: Instituto Nacional para el Estudio

de la Conciencia, 1994.

____________________. La meditación [versión Kindle].

Hidegar Laser. «La diferencia entre la luz láser y la luz tradicional», https://hidegar.com/es/diferencia-luz-laser-luz-tradicional/, accessed 24 August 2024.

Hölzel, B. K.; Carmody, J.; Vangel, M.; Congleton, C.; Yerramsetti, S. M.; Gard, T.; & Lazar, S. W. (2010). «Mindfulness practice leads to increases in regional brain gray matter density». Psychiatry Research: Neuroimaging, 191(1), pp. 36-43.

Icke, David. The Answer, Derby: Ickonic Publishing, 2022.

________. The Dream: The extraordinary revelation of who we are and where we are, Derby: Ickonic Publishing, 2023.

Inglis, Alexander James. The Principles of Secondary Education, London: Forgotten Books, 2012.

Jodorowsky, Alejandro; Costa, Mariana. Metagenealogía. Barcelona: Penguin Random House, 2009.

Khazan, Inna Y. The Clinical Handbook of Biofeedback: A step by Step guide for training and Practice with Mindfulness. West Sussex: Wiley Blackwell, 2013.

King, Stephen. On Writing - A Memoir of the Craft. New York: Scribner Classics, 2000.

Peterson, Jordan B. 12 Rules for Life: An antidote to chaos. Toronto: Penguin Random House of Canada, 2018.

Lazar, S. W.; Kerr, C. E.; Wasserman, R. H.; Gray, J. R.; Greve, D. N.; Treadway,

M. T.; & Fischl, B. (2005). «Meditation experience is associated with increased cortical thickness». NeuroReport, 16(17), pp. 1893-1897.

Leaf, Dr. Caroline. Enciende tu cerebro. Baker Publishing Group [versión Kindle].

Luders, E.; Clark, K.; Narr, K. L.; & Toga, A. W. (2011). «Enhanced brain connectivity in long-term meditation practitioners». NeuroImage, 57(4), pp. 1308-1316.

Newport, Cal. Deep Work: Rules for Focused Success in a Distracted World. New York: Grand Central Publishing, 2016.

Perlmutter, David. Brain Wash: Detox Your Mind for Clearer Thinking, Deeper Relationships and Lasting Happiness. Hodder & Stoughton [versión Kindle].

PFAS Central: «A project of green science policy (2024): PFAS-Free Products», https://pfascentral.org/pfas-free-products/, accessed 9 September 2024.

Public Health Madison & Dane County: https://publichealthmdc.com/es/salud-ambiental/peligros-ambientales/pfas/que-son-los-pfas#, accessed 9 September 2024.

Sanbonmatsu, T. et al. (2013): «Multitarea y la atención dividida», https://www.ncbi.nlm.nih.gov/pmc/articles/PMC5546942/, acceso 12 July 2024.

Strayer, D. et al. (2012): «Los efectos negativos del multitarea en el cerebro», https://www.nature.com/articles/s41583-022-00653-x, accessed 15 August 2024.

Reich, Wilhelm. Etter, God and Evil Cosmic Superimposition. Toronto: Doubleday Canada, 1973.

Riso, Walter. Los límites del amor. México: Editorial Océano, 2012.

Tang, Y. Y.; Ma, Y.; Wang, J.; Fan, Y.; Feng, S.; Lu, Q.; & Posner, M. I. (2007). «Short-term meditation training improves attention and self-regulation». Proceedings of the National Academy of Sciences, 104(43), pp. 17152-17156.

Twenge, J. M.; & Campbell, W. K. (2018). «Association of Screen Time and Depression in Adolescence». Journal of the American Medical Association Pediatrics, 172(5), pp. 417-424.

Take back the leadership of your mind

The Success MINDSET

Paola Knecht

DISCOVER YOUR POWER,
HEAL YOUR LIFE, CHANGE THE WORLD
AWAKEN
YOUR
INNER
GENIE
PAOLA KNECHT

INCLUDES A PRACTICAL 30-DAY GUIDE
TO MOVE FROM CHAOS TO LASTING HABITS
ORGANIZE
YOUR MIND,
TRANSFORM
YOUR LIFE
PAOLA KNECHT

A World of Illusions

A Wake-Up Call and the Search for the Truth

PAOLA KNECHT

www.ingramcontent.com/pod-product-compliance
Lightning Source LLC
Chambersburg PA
CBHW071347230926
51846CB00002B/476

9783952628317